HANDBOOK OF INSECT BIOLOGY

HANDBOOK OF INSECT BIOLOGY

By

Dr. Guruprasad B.R.

Post-doctoral Research Associate
Central Food Technology & Research Institute
Mysore (India)

&

Dr. Anand Krishna Tiwari

Assistant Professor
School of Biological Sciences & Biotechnology
Indian Institute of Advanced Research
Koba, Gandhinagar –382 007
Gujarat (India)

DPH

DISCOVERY PUBLISHING HOUSE PVT. LTD.
NEW DELHI-110 002

Published by:

Namit Wasan

DISCOVERY PUBLISHING HOUSE PVT. LTD.

4383/4B, Ansari Road, Darya Ganj

New Delhi-110 002 (India)

Phone : +91-11-23279245; 23253475; 43596065

E-mail : discoverybooksindia@gmail.com
discoverypublishinghouse@gmail.com
namitwasan9@gmail.com

web : www.discoverypublishinggroup.com

***First Edition:* 2011**

ISBN: 978-81-8356-910-1

Handbook of Insect Biology

Dedicated
To my
Parents, Teachers
and
Friends

Preface

Insects are beautiful creatures on this mother planet with huge number of varieties. Probably insects are known for pollination of many different species of plants, which is a process that has been adapted over millions of years by both parties. This process simply couldn't function without insects, particularly bees, butterflies and the like, who each pollinate thousands of flowers in their short lifetimes. Even with the intervention of scientific methods of pollination, mankind would not be able to keep up with the work done by these pollen and nectar feeders. So as a result many of the different colors, patterns and shaped that we sec in nature today are a direct result of insects. Soma insects are harmful to human and food too, but not all

The intension of this book is to give knowledge on insects which come across in our daily life and also play important role in our life of mankind. Another important things that insects have been used for is experimentation for modern science using live subjects. Due to the fact that certain chemicals can't realistically be used on either humans or animals for cruelty reasons, insects often make good test subjects. Also the fact that they are more simplistic than animals means that scientists can better understand the effects of experiments on insects over longer periods.

Due to most insects short life spans experiments can also be done over the course of multiple generations much faster than it could be even with lab mice.

The present work was undertaken to give information regarding insect to all class of the people. This book is more informative especially on some particular insects which commonly found around us. This is very useful for Students those who are interested in entomology.

Guruprasad B.R
Anand K. Tiwari

Contents

1 Insect

General Introduction

One of the most beautiful creatures in the world is insect. The insects are among the most diverse group of animals on the planet and include more than a million described species and represent more than half of all known living organisms. The word Insects is from Latin *insectum* are a class within the arthropods covered by exoskeleton, made up chitin of with three-part body (head, thorax, and abdomen), three pairs of jointed legs. So they belong to phylum Arthopoda, compound eyes, and two antennae. They number of extant species is estimated at between six and ten million. Potentially represent over 90 per cent of the differing metazoan life forms on Earth. Insects may be found in nearly all environments, they are cosmopolitan in nature, although only a small number of species occur in the oceans, a habitat dominated by another arthropoda group, the crustaceans. Class Insecta are a major division and most diverse group of animals on the earth belonging to arthropods with over a million number of species and largest in number among the animal combined.

Insects are cosmopolitan may be found in nearly all environments on our planet, although some are found in extreme environment and also in deep ocean. There are approximately 6,500 dragonfly species, 171,000 butterfly and moth, 120,000 fly, 20,000 grasshopper, 82,000 true bug, 360,000 beetle, and 110,000 bee, wasp and ant species described to date. Some species are not yet discovered properly, which range from two million to 50 million, with newer studies favouring a lower figure of about six to ten million. Adult modern insects range in size from a 0.139 millimetre Mymarid wasp (*Dicopomorpha echmepterygis*) to a 55.5 centimetre long Stick insect (*Phobaeticus serratipes*). The heaviest reported insect is a Giant Weta (at 70 grams), controversy to this there are possible candidates include the *Goliathus goliatus*, *Goliathus regius*, *Goliath beetles* and *Titanus giganteus*, but the actual size is not yet confirmed truly.

Most of the insect starts their life from the eggs. Insect growth is constrained by the inelastic exoskeleton and also includes a series of molts. The immature stages are entirely differ from the adults in structure, habit and habitat and can include a passive pupal stage in those groups that undergo complete metamorphosis. Insects which undergo incomplete metamorphosis they lack a pupal stage and adults develop through nymphal stages. The higher level relationship of the hexapoda is unclear. Fossilized insects of enormous size have been found from the Paleozoic Era, including giant dragonflies with wingspans of 50 to 75 cm. According to the evolutionist they are evolved along with flowering plants.

Insects are mostly solitary, but some insects, such as bees, ants, and termites are social and live in large, well-organized colonies. Some insects, such as earwigs, show maternal care, guarding their eggs and young. Insects can communicate with each other in a variety of ways. Male moths can sense the pheromones of female moths over distances of many kilometres. Other species communicate with sounds: crickets stridulate, or rub their wings together, to attract a mate and repel other males. Lampyridae in the beetle order Coleoptera communicate with light. Humans regard certain insects as pests and attempt to control them using insecticides and pesticides and a host of other techniques. Some insects damage crops by feeding on sap, leaves or fruits, a few bite humans and livestock, alive and dead, to feed on blood and some are capable of transmitting diseases to humans, pets and livestock. Many other insects are considered ecologically beneficial and a few provide direct economic benefit. Silkworms and bees have been domesticated by humans for the production of silk and honey.

Insects typically move about by walking, flying or occasionally sinking and swimming at the same time. Because it allows for rapid yet stable movement, many insects adopt a tripedal gait in which they walk with their legs touching the ground in alternating triangles. Insects are the only invertebrates to have evolved flight. Many insects spend at least part of their life underwater, with larval adaptations that include gills and some adult insects are aquatic and have adaptations for swimming (mosquitoes). Some species, like water striders, are capable of walking on the surface of water too.

Morphology and Physiology

The morphology of insects enables the phenomenal success of this class of arthropods. The quantity and diversity of its classification are matched by a large variation of modifications in its body structure. Speciation, short generations and long lineage have caused insects to evolve in many ways resulting in very large variations in morphology. These modifications allow insects to occupy almost every good ecological niche, and taste variety of food sources and possess diverse lifestyles. Insect body sizes range from 0.3 mm in the case of wasps which parasitise insect eggs to the 30 cms wingspan of the American owlet moth *Thysania agrippina*) is a large moth in the Noctuidae family. It has a wingspan of up to 12 inches (31 cm), making it the Lepidopteran with the biggest wingspan found in Central and South.

Insects are by far the most successful group in Arthropoda. They differ in significant ways from the other classes of Hexapoda, such as Protura, Collembola and others) who are now considered by some authorities to be more basal than insects. Morphology was the main source for inputs for constructing insect phylogeny, but was invariably beset with conjecture and conditionality. A stable and reliable phylogeny of insects is slowly developing due to the advent of DNA genome analysis. This has reduced the importance of morphology in evolutionary studies. However morphology still plays a great part in understanding how insects are adapt and having marvelous lifestyles on this planet.

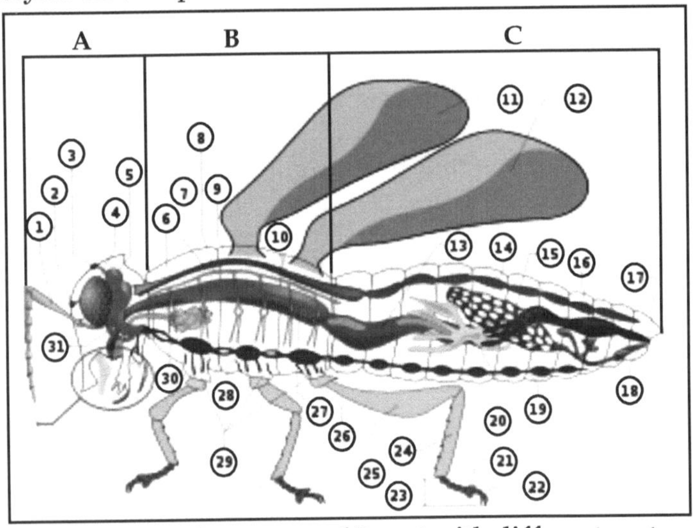

Fig. 1.1: **Internal structure of Insect with different parts**

***A*- Head *B*- Thorax *C*- Abdomen**

1. Antenna; 2. Ocelli (Lower); 3. Ocelli (Upper); 4. Compound Eye; 5. Brain (Cerebral Ganglia); 6. Prothorax; 7. Dorsal Blood Vessel; 8. Tracheal Tubes (Trunk with Spiracle); 9. Mesothorax; 10. Metathorax; 11. Forewing; 12. Hindwing; 13. Mid-gut (Stomach); 14. Dorsal Tube (Heart); 15. Ovary; 16. Hind-gut; (Intestine, Rectum & Anus); 17. Anus; 18. Oviduct; 19. Nerve Chord (Abdominal Ganglia); 20. Malpighian Tubes; 21. Tarsal Pads; 22. Claws; 23. Tarsus; 24. Tibia; 25. Femur; 26. Trochanter; 27. Fore-gut (Crop, Gizzard); 28. Thoracic Ganglion; 29. Coxa; 30. Salivary Gland; 31. Subesophageal Ganglion; 32. Mouthparts

Body of Insect

Insects have segmented bodies supported by an exoskeleton, a hard outer covering made mostly of chitin. The segments of the body are organized into three distinctive but interconnected by tagmata: a head, a thorax, and an abdomen. The head supports a pair of sensory antennae, a pair of compound eyes, and, if present, one to three simple eyes (or ocelli) and three sets of variously modified appendages that form the mouthparts. The thorax has six segmented legs one pair each for the prothorax, mesothorax and the metathorax segments making up the thorax and, if present in the species, two or four wings. The abdomen consists of eleven segments, though in a few species of insects these segments may be fused together or reduced in size. The abdomen also contains most of the digestive, respiratory, excretory and reproductive internal structures. There is considerable variation and many adaptations in the body parts of insects especially wings, legs, antenna, mouth-parts etc.

Insects are the only non-chordata to have developed flight capability, and this has played an important role in their success. These muscles are able to contract multiple times for each single nerve impulse, allowing the wings to beat faster than would ordinarily be possible. Having their muscles attached to their exoskeletons is more efficient and allows more muscles connections; crustaceans also use the same method, though all spiders use hydraulic pressure to extend their legs, a system inherited from their pre-arthropod ancestors. Unlike insects, though, most aquatic crustaceans are biomineralized with calcium carbonate extracted from the water. Their outer skeleton of the insect is known as cuticle and made up of the made up of two layers:

1. the upper layer epicuticle, which is a thin and waxy water resistant outer layer and contains no chitin; and
2. a lower layer called the procuticle.

The procuticle is chitinous and much thicker than the epicuticle it is made up of two layers: an outer layer known as the exocuticle and an inner layer known as the endocuticle. The tough and flexible endocuticle is built from numerous layers of fibrous chitin and proteins, criss-crossing each others in a sandwich pattern, while the exocuticle is rigid and hardened. The exocuticle is greatly reduced in many soft-bodied insects especially during their larval stages. (e.g., caterpillars).

Generally nervous system of an insect can be divided into a brain and a ventral nerve cord. In the head there is a presence of capsule which is fused with six segments, each with a pair of ganglia, or a cluster of nerve cells outside of the brain. The first three pairs of ganglia are fused into the brain, while the three following pairs are fused into a structure of three pairs of ganglia under the insect's esophagus, called the subesophageal ganglion.

The thoracic segments have one ganglion on each side, which are connected into a pair, one pair per segment. This arrangement is also seen in the abdomen but only in the first eight segments. Many species of insects have reduced numbers of ganglia due to fusion or reduction. Some cockroaches have just six ganglia in the abdomen, whereas the wasp the European hornet (*Vespa crabro*) commonly known simply as the "hornet", is the largest European eusocial wasp. The queen measures 25 to 35 mm (1-1.4 in) long; males and workers are smaller. In males, as in most members of the Aculeata, the antennae have 13 segments, while in females there are only 12; also as in other aculeates, the male abdomen has seven visible segments, while the female has six; females possess an ovipositor modified into a sting which is not barbed. See wasp and bee characteristics to help identify similar insects.

This has only two in the thorax and three in the abdomen. Some insects, like the house fly *Musca domestica*,

The housefly (common housefly), *Musca domestica*, is a Diptera order of the Brachycera suborder. It is the most common of all domestic flies, accounting for about 90 per cent of all flies in human habitations, and indeed one of the most widely distributed insects, found all over the world; it is considered a pest that can carry serious diseases having all the body ganglia fused into a single large thoracic ganglion.

Insects have nociceptors, a sensory receptor that reacts to potentially damaging stimuli by sending nerve signals to the spinal cord and brain. This process, called nociception, usually causes the perception of pain. Their cells that detect and transmit sensations of pain. This was discovered in 2003 by studying the variation in reactions of larvae of the common fruitfly *Drosophila* to the touch of a heated probe and an unheated one. The larvae reacted to the touch of the heated probe with a stereotypical rolling behavior that was not exhibited when the larvae were touched by the unheated probe. Although nociception has been demonstrated in insects, there is not a consensus that insects feel pain consciously.

An insect as well developed digestive system to extract nutrients and other substances from the food it consumes some insects are omnivores. Most of this food is ingested in the form of complex macromolecules and other substances like proteins, polysaccharides, fats, and nucleic acids. These macromolecules must be broken down by catabolic reactions into smaller molecules like simple sugars and amino acids before being used by cells of the body for energy, growth, or reproduction. This break-down process is known as digestion. The main structure of an insect's digestive system is a long enclosed tube called the 'alimentary canal', which runs lengthwise through the body. The alimentary canal directs food unidirectionally from the mouth to the anus. It has three sections, each of which performs a different process of digestion. In addition to the alimentary canal, insects also have paired salivary glands and salivary reservoirs. These structures usually reside in the thorax, adjacent to the foregut.

Insect also produce saliva in their mouth produce by the salivary gland. The salivary ducts lead from the glands to the reservoirs and then forward through the head to an opening called the salivarium, located behind the hypopharynx. By moving its mouthparts, the insect can mix its food with saliva. The mixture of saliva and food then travels through the salivary tubes into the mouth, where it begins to break. Some insects, like flies, have extra-oral digestion. Insects using extra-oral digestion expel digestive enzymes onto their food to break it down. This strategy allows insects to extract a significant proportion of the available nutrients from the food source. The gut is where almost all of insects digestion takes place. Digestive system was divided into the foregut, midgut and hindgut.

The first section of the alimentary canal is the foregut. The foregut is line with a cuticular lining made of chitin and proteins as protection from tough food. The foregut includes the buccal cavity (mouth), pharynx, esophagus, and crop and proventriculus (any part may be highly modified) which both store food and signify when to continue passing onward to the midgut. Here, digestion starts as partially chewed food is broken down by and mixed with saliva from the salivary glands. As the salivary glands produce fluid and carbohydrate-digesting enzymes (mostly amylases), strong muscles in the pharynx pump fluid into the buccal cavity, lubricating the food like the salivarium does, This type of mechanism is commonly found in the blood feeders and xylem and phloem feeders after pharynx there is a presence of esophagus, which is just a simple tube called crop after the crop some insects possess gizzard which act like a grinder for mixing the food as much as possible during the digestion. In some insects after the presence of the crop there is a structure called proventriculus. Next part is midgut where the majority of digestion takes place. There is a Microscopic in the midgut, called microvilli. This increase the surface of absorption of the nutrients of the nutrient. In some insects, the role of the microvilli and where they are located may vary. Simultaneously there are microvilli which can produce digestive system. Hind gut is last part of the alimentary canal where the undigested food particles are stored mostly the fecal pellets and uric acid. This uric acid is formed by the hemolymph waste products. In the hind gut there is the presence of the malphigian tubules, Malphigian tubules is the junction between midgut and hindgut. This malphigian tubules which act as the kidney in higher mammals. The last part of the hindgut is the rectum which is the responsible for defecation.

Structure of Malpighian Tubules

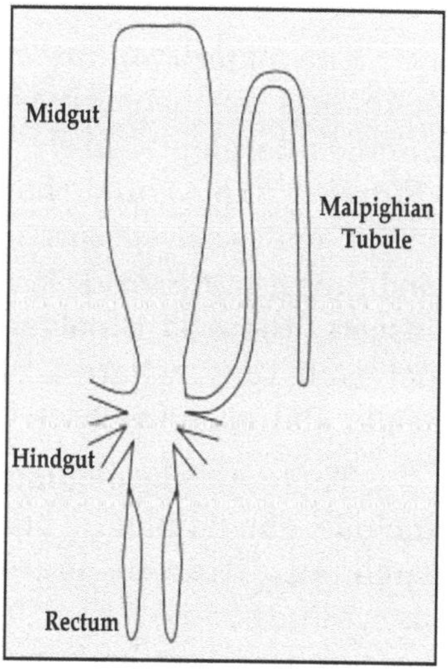

Respiration of insect is through a special type system of internal tubes and sacs where gas can enter by trachea. Since oxygen is delivered directly, the circulatory system is not used to carry oxygen, and is therefore greatly reduced. The circulatory system of insect does not possess veins or arteries, and instead consists of little more than a single, perforated dorsal tube which pulses peristaltically. Towards the thorax, the dorsal tube divides into chambers and acts like the insect's heart. The opposite end of the dorsal tube is like the aorta of the insect circulating the hemolymph, this is anlog to the animal blood, inside the body cavity. Air is taken in through openings on the sides of the abdomen called 'spiracles'.

There are many different patterns of gas exchange demonstrated by different groups of insects. Gas exchange patterns in insects can range from continuous and diffusive ventilation, to discontinuous gas exchange. During continuous gas exchange, oxygen is taken in and carbon dioxide is released in a continuous cycle, where as in discontinuous gas exchange, however, the insect takes in oxygen while it is active and small amounts of carbon dioxide are released when the insect is at rest. Diffusive ventilation is simply a form of continuous gas exchange that occurs by diffusion rather than physically taking in the oxygen. Some species of insect that are submerged also have adaptations to aid in respiration. As larvae, many insects have gills that can extract oxygen dissolved in water, while others need to rise to the water surface to replenish air supplies which may be held or trapped in special structures.

The majority of insects hatch from eggs. Some species of insects are ovoviviparous. The eggs of ovoviviparous animals develop entirely inside the female Ex: Cockroach (*Blaptica dubia*), and then hatch immediately upon being laid. Some other species are viviparous (genus Diploptera), and thus gestate inside the mother and are born alive. Some insects, there is a polyembronic nature Ex wasps show polyembryony, where a single fertilized egg divides into many and in some cases thousands of separate embryos.

There are developmental and reproductive variations include haplodiploidy, polymorphism, sexual dimorphism such as different male and female ex *Drosophila*, parthenogenesis (in honey bee) and more rarely hermaphroditism both male and female part are present in the single animal. In haplodiploidy, this is a condition where sex is determined by the chromosomes (wasps). Polymorphism is the where a species may have different look and forms that is different colour pattern example *D. nasuta* and *D. melanogaster*. Paedomorphosis this is seen in some insects may retain phenotypes visible character that are commonly seen in normal juveniles; Parthenogenesis is a phenomenon where there unfertilized eggs of female can hatch into young ones, Many aphids undergo a form of parthenogenesis, called cyclical parthenogenesis, in which they alternate between one or many generations of asexual and sexual reproduction. More rarely, insects display hermaphroditism, in which a given individual has both male and female reproductive organs. Some Insects are adapted to cold and dry conditions. Some temperate region insects are capable of activity during winter, while some others may migrate or go into a state of torpor. There are the insect undergoes diapause during unfavourable condition.

During life cycle insects undergo the different type of the metomorphosis where there is a series of the molts. The molting process begins as the insect's epidermis secretes a new epicuticle. After this new epicuticle is secreted, the epidermis releases a mixture of enzymes that digests the endocuticle and thus detaches the old cuticle. When this stage is complete, the insect makes its body swell by taking in a large quantity of water or air, which makes the old cuticle split along predefined weaknesses where the old exocuticle was thinnest and metamorphosis are two type that may be incomplete and complete metamorphosis. Incomplete metomorphosis is as called hemimetabolim. The insect which under go the incomplete metamorphosis are called 'Nymph'.

Sexual Selection

According to Charles Darwin the sexual selection can be expressed by intraspecific competition. He stated sexual selection is due to struggle between the individuals of one sex, generally the males, for the possession of the other sex" Today biologist differentiate the sexual selection with number of terms like male choice (it is usually males who fight each other), female choice and multiple choice experiments Traits selected by male combat are called secondary sexual characteristics this is one of the characters commonly demonstrated in insects such as Wasps and *Drosophila*.

> *The sexual struggle is of two kinds: in the one it is between the individuals of the same sex, generally the males, in order to drive away or kill their rivals, the females remaining passive; while in the other, the struggle is likewise between the individuals of the same sex, in order to excite or charm those of the opposite sex, generally the females, which no longer remain passive, but select the more agreeable partners.*
>
> *–Charles Darwin, 1871*

Do Insect Sense and Communicate

Most of the insects have are very sensitive organs for the perception. Some insects are going to select their mate with help of the pheromones of female moths over distances of many kilometers. In the same manner some insect are going to perceive the ultraviolet rays example bees. There are a variety of different mechanisms by which insects sense sound, but the ways are not universal, insects can generally hear sound if they can produce it. Different insect species can have varying hearing, though most insects can hear only a narrow range of frequencies related to the frequency of the sounds they can produce. Like mosquitoes have been found to hear up to 2 to 2.5 MHz. Some variries of grasshoppers can hear up to 50 MHz. There are some predatory insects can detect the sound produced by the prey. Example some nocturnal moths can perceive the ultrasonic emissions of bats, which helps them avoid predation.

Some insects like wasps are going to sense the number of the species present in the colony. In case of the wasps mother can lay the eggs in each cells and provide the larva for feeding the young one. In case of the *Drosophila* the different species produce different communication during the sexual activity. Even cockroach is one of the nocturnal insects which can sense the type of the food even in the darkness and it will prefer the food which is omnivorous like same manner insect communicate with light in case of *Drosophila* under go mating during early morning (sun rise) between 6 am to 11 am and compare to the other time of the same day. In the same case of the *Drosophila* which are opposite to geotropic in nature they are not so active in darkness and phototropic in nature.

Insects Produce the Light Production and Vision?

The insects have eyes for the sight seeing they possesses compound eyes and some insect are possess the simple eyes two made up of the ocelli and the size of the eyes are going to vary in number and two antennae. some insect are going to see the objects and enemies and can under go the diapause. some families of insect such as Mycetophilidae (Diptera), Lampyridae, Phengodidae, Poduridae, Elateridae and Staphylinidae are biolumine-scent. and Lampyridae which consists the fire flies are capable of the production of the their own light and generates the falshes these are traits which are useful in the attract the mates. Many species are able to detect light in the infrared, ultraviolet and the visible light wavelengths. differentiated color vision has been demonstrated in many species and the phylogenetic analysis suggests that UV-green-blue trichromacy existed from at least the Devonian period between 416 and 359 million years ago.

Can Insect make Noise and Hearing?

Some insects are going to produce and sense the sound. Insects produce sound with help of their appendages. In case of the grasshopper there is the stridualtion action is seen and in case of the *Drosophila* different species produce different sound to attract mates. Especially the male flies are going to produce different noice such as vibration through the wing and there are capable of the producing the noice as much as possible. *Drosophila rajasekari* is going to produce the different action like circling licking tapping and extruding done by the female flies. *Drosophila* during the sexual intercources going to exhibit different actions such as tapping, scissoring, licking (male) and escaping (female) during in that situation they are going to produce some noise. Silk worm (*Bombyx mori*) which commonly seen in India also make noise during the larval conditions when there were rearing in rearing plates during cutting the *Morus alba* leaf for there development they make lot of noise even in the dark condition. The African cicada *Brevisana brevis* has been measured at 106.7 decibels at a distance of 50 cm (20 in). Some insects, such as the hawk moths and butterflies, can hear ultrasound and they take sudden action evasive action. Some moths produce ultrasonic clicks that were once thought to have a role in jamming bat echolocation. Some otherwise palatable moths have evolved to mimic these calls. Some group of the insects such as Coleoptera, Hymenoptera, Lepidoptera, Mantodea, and Neuroptera produces the sound these sounds are going to warn the other insects. Tympanal organs are the organs that can perceive the sounds some insects are known to communicate via underwater sounds such as species in Hemiptera the corixids water boatmen. For example, an insect is caught in a spider web and struggles to escape. Those vibrations it produces are sensed by the spider, who is alerted to its presence. Through these vibrations, the spider can tell where on the web the insect is located.

Some species use vibrations for communicating within members of the same species, such as to attract mates as in the songs of the shield bug (*Nezara viridula*). Vibrations can also be used to communicate between entirely different species; lycaenid (gossamer-winged butterfly) caterpillars which are myrmecophilous (living in a mutualistic association with ants) communicate with ants in this way.

The Madagascar hissing cockroach has the ability to press air through its spiracles to make a hissing noise as a sign of aggression the Death's-head Hawkmoth makes a squeaking noise by forcing air out of their pharynx when agitated, which may also reduce aggressive worker honey bee behavior when the two are in close proximity.

Social Behaviour

Insects are generally social animals they live in group such as termites ants, bees and also wasps. They live together in large colonies these colonies are well organized and characterized that may be so tightly integrated and genetically similar that the colonies of some species are sometimes considered dominant organisms. It is sometimes argued that the various species of honey bee are the only invertebrates (and indeed one of the few non-human groups) to have evolved a system of abstract symbolic communication where a behavior is used to represent and convey specific information about something in the environment. During the communication honey bee perform the dance language. This type of the language is helpful in the insect to identify the nectar. Only insects which live in nests or colonies demonstrate any true capacity for fine-scale spatial orientation or homing. This can allow an insect to return unerringly to a single hole a few millimeters in diameter among thousands of apparently identical holes clustered together, after a trip of up to several kilometers' distance. In a phenomenon known as philopatry, Insects which undergoes the diphase have shown the ability to recall a specific location up to a year after last viewing the area of interest. Some of the insects seasonally migrate large distances between different geographic regions.

Care of Young Ones

The life span of the insects is very short this type of the character are also depends upon the species of the insects. During there life span some insects are going to exhibit some form of parental care, where they will at least guard their eggs, and sometimes continue guarding their offspring until adulthood, and possibly even feeding them. Another simple form of parental care is to construct a nest (a burrow or an actual construction, either of which may be simple or complex), store provisions in it, and lay an egg upon those provisions. The adult does not contact the growing offspring, but it nonetheless does provide food. This sort of care is typical of bees and various types of wasps.

Locomotion Flight insects have well developed wings for the flight and the shape of the wing may vary depend upon there habitat. Wing is the most important trait in evolution. Eventually, so many theories which explain the wing development and evolution. They are paranotal lobes and epicoxa theory. Some entomologists suggest that the wings are from paranotal lobes, or extensions from the insect's exoskeleton called the nota, called the *paranotal theory*. Other theories are based on a pleural origin. The pleuron is membrane on the sides of the thorax. These theories include suggestions that wings originated from modified gills, spiracular flaps or as from an appendage of the epicoxa. The *epicoxal theory* suggests the insect wings are modified epicoxal exites, a modifed appendage at the base of the legs or coxa. In the Carboniferous age, some of the *Meganeura* dragonflies had as much as a 50 cm (20 in) wide wingspan. The appearance of gigantic insects has been found to be consistent with high atmospheric oxygen. The respiratory system of insects constrains their size; however the high oxygen in the atmosphere allowed larger sizes. The largest flying insects today are much smaller and include several moth species such as the Atlas moth and the White Witch (*Thysania agrippina*). Insect flight has been a topic of great interest in aerodynamics due partly to the inability of steady-state theories to explain the lift generated by the tiny wings of insects.

Walking

Many adult insects use six legs for walking and have adopted a tripedal gait. The tripedal gait allows for rapid walking while always having a stable stance and has been studied extensively in cockroaches. The legs are used in alternate triangles touching the ground. For the first step, the middle right leg and the front and rear left legs are in contact with the ground and move the insect forward, while the front and rear right leg and the middle left leg are lifted and moved forward to a new position. When they touch the ground to form a new stable triangle the other legs can be lifted and brought forward in turn and so on. The purest form of the tripedal gait is seen in insects moving at high speeds. However, this type of locomotion is not rigid and insects can adapt a variety of gaits. For example, when moving slowly, turning, or avoiding obstacles, four or more feet may be touching the ground. Insects can also adapt their gait to cope with the loss of one or more limbs.

Cockroaches are among the fastest insect runners and, at full speed, adopt a bipedal run to reach a high velocity in proportion to their body size. As cockroaches move very quickly, they need to be video recorded at several hundred frames per second to reveal their gait. More sedate locomotion is seen in the stick insects or walking sticks (Phasmatodea). A few insects have evolved to walk on the surface of the water, especially the bugs of the Gerridae family, commonly known as water striders. A few species of ocean-skaters in the genus *Halobates* even live on the surface of open oceans, a habitat that has few insect species.

Use in Robotics

Today man as learnt to fly huge height and vast distance through air bus. This idea is from the wing of the insects. Insect walking is of particular interest as an alternative form of locomotion in robots. The study of insects and bipeds has a significant impact on possible robotic methods of transport. This may allow new robots to be designed that can traverse terrain that robots with wheels may be unable to handle.

Evolution

What is the reason for the variety of insects on our planet? The answer is very simple that is decent with modification or evolution. There is no clear picture for the evolution of the insect with other animals Although more traditionally grouped with millipedes and centipedes, evidence has emerged favoring closer evolutionary ties with crustaceans. In the Pancrustacea theory, insects, together with Remipedia and Malacostraca, make up a natural clade. Other terrestrial arthropods, such as centipedes, millipedes, scorpions and spiders, are sometimes confused with insects since their body plans can appear similar, sharing (as do all arthropods) a jointed exoskeleton. However, upon closer examination their features differ significantly; most noticeably they do not have the six legs characteristic of adult insects.

Insects and Ecosystem

In ecosystem insects are never primary producers, they are important primary, secondary and even tertiary consumers in some ecosystem. Moreover, they are fundamental participants as shredders in the decomposition process in terrestrial and aquatic ecosystems. Blowflies and flesh flies (Diptera: Calliphoridae and Sarcophagidae, respectively) are well known insect decomposers whose larvae often feed within carrion or excrement. Likewise, carrion beetles (Coleoptera: Silphidae) of the genus Necrophorus excavate chambers beneath the dead bodies of small mammals. Perhaps the most impressive decomposers in the insect world are the termites.

The type of insect pest capable of disseminating diseases from one mammalian host to another or from one plant to another is called vectors. Insects are well known vectors of some of the local and global epidemics such as dreaded diseases like malaria, dengue, sleeping sickness, plague and encephalitis. Malaria is estimated to infect around 300 million people in the world. Though dipterans dominate as vectors of a number of human and livestock diseases, other members of the orders such as Hemiptera (true bugs) and Siphonaptera (fleas) also profoundly play their role making enormous impact by spreading epidemics such as bubomic plague (black death).

Natural ecosystem throughout the world is being severely altered by human interventions. Population pressure bring about the establishment of unplanned human colonization, migration, construction of hydroelectric dams, irrigation projects, open pit, agricultural development etc. Such activities often favor the propagation of mosquitoes as well and spread vector borne diseases. Throughout the recent history, the tropical region of the world have been affected more severely by infectious diseases than the temperate world. Much of the outbreaks of diseases in these regions are due to both biological and environmental factors that encourage vector breeding. Therefore, the study of the relationships between humans, vectors and pathogens and their ecology with respect to disease transmission, is important.

History of Entomological Warfare

History of the entomological warfare was date back to 14th century, where there was a out break of the plague in the Asia this situation was also describe as a entomological war by some of the historian and thinkers, it was describe as Black death. This was spread to Crimean city of Kaffa this was also described as a biological attack. There was also incident of using the bees and comb of bees are thrown to the place of the enemies. There is the example of biological warfare in World War II, where there was a use of Colorado potato beetle (*Lepinotarsa decemlineata*), as biological weapons this beetle was suggested by the Germany. The beetle was first found in Germany in 1914, as an invasive species from North America. There are no records that indicate the beetle was ever employed as a weapon by Germany or any other nation during the war. Regardless, the Germans had developed plans to drop the beetles on English crops. Although there are reports that the Germany tested the beetles as weaponization programme where they released 54,000 of the bettles. In 1944, an infestation of Colorado potato beetles was reported in Germany. The source of the infestation is unknown; speculation has offered three alternative theories as to the origin of the infestation. One option is Allied action, an entomological attack, another is that it was the result of the German testing, and still another more likely explanation is that it was merely a natural occurrence. It was Canada started to use the vector borne warfare and this was followed by the Japan to developing the plague fleas as a weapon then the United States followed this manner. Dr. G.B. Reed, of United States was concentrating the biological weapons in his research on mosquito vectors, biting flies, and plague infected fleas during World War II. This was confirmed in the: *Secrets from the Early Cold War and Korea* by Endicott, Stephen, and Hagermann, Edward. There are the incidents of the warfare of the biological weapon used by the Japan and its military systems. The Japanese military dispersed the insects by spraying them from low-flying airplanes and dropping bombs filled with a mixture of insects and disease. Localized and deadly epidemics resulted and nearly 500,000 Chinese died of disease. An "international symposium" of historians declared in 2002 that Japanese entomological warfare in China was responsible for the deaths of 440,000.

According to the scientist J.B.S Haldane suggested that the Britain and Germany were both vulnerable to entomological attack through the Colorado potato beetle. In 1942 the United States shipped 15,000 Colorado potato beetles to Britain for study as a weapon. The Soviet Union was also contributed to Biological warfare programme where they develop the techniques for insects to transmit animal pathogens such as Foot and Mouth disease for this they used ticks for the transmission. This nation also used avian ticks to transmit *Chlamydophila psittaci* to chickens. During the 1950s the United States conducted a series of field tests using entomological weapons. Operation Big Itch, in 1954, was designed to test munitions loaded with uninfected fleas (*Xenopsylla cheopis*). In May 1955 over 300,000 yellow fever mosquitoes (*Aedes aegypti*) were dropped over parts of the (U.S.) Georgia to determine if the air-dropped mosquitoes could survive to take meals from humans by Rose, William 1981. The mosquito tests were known as Operation Big Buzz. The U.S. engaged in at least two other EW testing programs Operation Drop Kick and Operation May Day. A 1981 Army report outlined these tests as well as multiple cost-associated issues that occurred with EW. The report is partially declassified—some information is blacked out, including everything concerning "Drop Kick" — and included "cost per death" calculations ("An Introduction to Biological Weapons, Their Prohibition, and the Relationship to Biosafety", *The Sunshine Project*, April 2002). The cost per death, according to the report, for a vector-borne biological agent achieving a 50 per cent mortality rate in an attack on a city was $0.29 in 1976 dollars. Such an attack was estimated to result in 625,000 deaths. These are concepts which are seen in the history of the insect where the insects are used as the biological weapons.

In 1972 there was a Biological and Toxic Weapons Convention where it was failed to come to conclusion about the biological weapons. This treaty does not the cover the vectors as biological weapons. There was Article 1 where there is the ban of the "Weapons, equipment or means of delivery designed to use such agents or toxins for hostile purposes or in armed conflict."

In some instants the insects are commonly used as entomological warfare (EW) and used to attack enemies, this idea was started from centuries and research and development have continued into the modern era. The EW has been used in battle by Japan and several other nations have developed and been accused of using an entomological warfare program. Entomological warfare is a type of biological warfare that uses insects in as direct attack or vectors to deliver the biological agent such as anthrax species. Entomological warfare is three types they are:

1. Release the uninfected bees to the areas where enemies are located.
2. Release of the insects which are infected with a pathogens where enemies are located overnight.
3. Release of the insects which can affect the areas of agriculture and crops

Insects Trouble to Humankind

According to the entomologists insects originated during 450million years ago that is the time of the Devonian period. Diptera, the insect class order which appeared not later than triassic period, about 200 million years ago. This was the time the insects like mosquitoes aroused. The most common species of the mosquitoes during this period is *Culex.* The first fossil of the mosquitoes was recognized the quaternary period (40-60 million years ago). Even today man is suffering lot from Insects that to from mosquitoes. Mosqitoes are major insects which are going to cause disease which can effect man in terms of many diseases. Mosquitoes act as vector and going to cause harmful example: *Chikunguanya.*

The evolutionary history of insects stretches back at least to the Devonian period, i.e., about 450 million years ago. Diptera, the insect order to which flies and mosquitoes belong, might have first appeared not later than the

Triassiac period, about 200 million years ago. Mosquitoes probably arose later in this same period, but the first fossil specimens recognizable as such are associated with the Eocene epoch of the quaternary period (40-60 million years ago). Some of those specimens look remarkably similar to present day *Culex* species. For little over a century, scientists have known that arthropods could serve as vectors and intermediate hosts of pathogens of humans and other vertebrate animals. Arthropods also can cause disease directly, for example allergic and secondary infections can occur due to severe scratching of the affected areas of the skin, particularly among children.

Diptera is the most important order of insects in medical entomology and mosquitoes belong to the family culicidae with about 3450 species in 37 genera. Some of the most important diseases transmitted by them are malaria, filariasis, Japanese encephalitis, yellow fever, dengue haemorrhagic fever (DHF), rift valley fever etc. Among the mosquito transmitted viral diseases in India, JE and dengue occupies an important public health positions.

2 Drosophila

Drosophila melanogaster (Meigen) is a species of Diptera, or the order of flies, in the family Drosophilidae. The species is commonly known as the *common fruit fly* or *vinegar fly* and *Cinderella of genetics*. It was started as model organism by Charles W. Woodworth, this species is one of the most commonly used model organisms in biology, including studies in genetics, physiology, microbial pathogenesis and life history evolution, molecular biology, toxicology because they are easy to take care of, breed quickly, and lay many eggs. In Australia flies belonging to the family *Tephritidae* are also called fruit flies, which are known as economic pests in fruit production.

Morphology of *Drosophila*

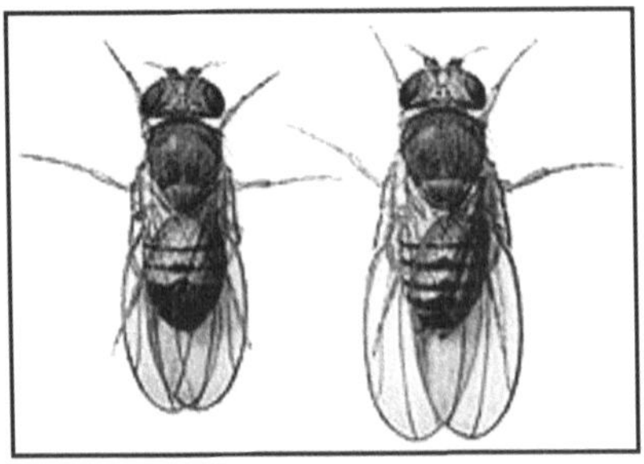

Male and female *D. melanogaster*

Today there are more than 3500 species of *Drosophila*. *Drosophila melanogaster* is commonly found in our kitchen and it is know as Domestic species especially in South India. Wildtype fruit flies have red eyes, the body is yellow-brown in colour, and have transverse black rings across their abdomen. Males are slightly smaller and the back of their bodies is darker. Males are easily distinguished from females based on colour differences, with a distinct black patch at the abdomen, less noticeable in recently emerged flies. They exhibit sexual dimorphism: females are about 2.5 millimetres (mm) (0.098 inches) long; and the sexcomb (a row of dark bristles on the tarsus of the first leg). Furthermore, males have a cluster of spiky hairs (claspers) surrounding the reproducing parts used to attach to the female during mating. Its genome is already sequence and found in the flybase website.

Reproduction and Life Cycle

The *D. melanogaster* lifespan is about 30 days at 29°C (84°F). The developmental period for *Drosophila melanogaster* varies with temperature, as with many ectothermic species. The shortest development time (egg to adult) is 7 days, is achieved at 23°C ± 22 °C. The development times increase at higher temperatures (20 days at 32 °C) due to heat stress. Under ideal conditions, the development time at 22 °C (77 °F) is 8.5 days, at 18 °C. Females lay some 400 eggs (embryos), about five at a time, into rotting fruit or other suitable material such as decaying mushrooms and sap fluxes. The eggs, which are about 0.5 millimetres long, hatch after 12-15 hours (at 25 °C or 77 °F). The resulting larvae grow for about 4 days (at 25 °C) there are two types of moulting (2nd- and 3rd-instar larvae), at about 24 and 48 h after hatching. During this time, they feed on the micro-organisms that decompose the fruit, as well as on the sugar of the fruit itself. Then the larvae proceeds for the puparium and undergo a four-day-long metamorphosis (at 25 °C), after which the adults eclose (emerge).

Females are ready to courting males at about 8-12 hours after emergence. Males perform a sequence of five behavioral patterns to court females. First, males orient themselves while playing a courtship song by horizontally extending and vibrating their wings. Soon after, the male positions itself at the rear of the female's abdomen in a low posture to tap and lick the female genitalia. Finally, the male curls its abdomen, and attempts copulation. Females can reject males by moving away and extruding their ovipositor. The average duration of successful copulation is 30 minutes, during which males transfer a few hundred very long (1.76 mm) sperm cells in seminal fluid to the female. Females store the sperm in a tubular receptacle and in two mushroom-shaped spermathecae, sperm from multiple matings compete for fertilization. A last male precedence is believed to exist in which the last male to mate with a female sires approximately 80 per cent of her offspring. This precedence was found to occur through displacement and incapacitation. Displacement is attributed to sperm handling by the female fly as multiple matings are conducted and is most significant during the first 1-2 days after copulation. Displacement from the seminal receptacle is more significant than displacement from the spermathecae. Incapacitation of first male sperm by second male sperm becomes significant 2-7 days after copulation. The seminal fluid of the second male is believed to be responsible for this incapacitation mechanism (without removal of first male sperm) which takes effect before fertilization occurs. The delay in effectiveness of the incapacitation mechanism is believed to be a protective mechanism that prevents a male fly from incapacitating its own sperm should it mate with the same female fly repetitively.

History of Use in Genetic Analysis

Today *Drosophila* is one of the most widely used and genetically best-known among all eukaryotic organisms. *Drosophila melanogaster* was among the first organism used for genetic analysis, and all organisms use common genetic systems; therefore, genetic processes such as transcription and replication in fruit flies helps in understanding these processes in other eukaryotes, including humans. Charles W. Woodworth is credited with being the first to breed Drosophila in quantity and for suggesting to W.E. Castle that they might be used for genetic research during his time at Harvard University. But it was not until 1910 that Thomas Hunt Morgan began using fruit flies in experimental studies of heredity at Columbia University. Morgan's laboratory was located on the top floor of Schermerhorn Hall, which became known as the Fly Room. The Fly Room was cramped with eight desks, each occupied by students and their experiments. They started off experiments using milk bottles to rear the fruit flies and handheld lenses for observing their traits. The lenses were later replaced by microscopes which enhanced their observations. The Fly Room was the source of some of the most important research in the history of biology. Morgan and his students eventually elucidated many basic principles of heredity, including sex-linked inheritance, epistasis, multiple alleles, and gene mapping.

Thomas Hunt Morgan and colleagues extended Mendel's work by describing x-linked inheritance and by showing that genes located on the same chromosome do not show independent assortment. Studies of x-linked traits helped confirm that genes are found on chromosomes, while studies of linked traits led to the first maps showing the locations of genetic loci on chromosomes". The first maps of *Drosophila* chromosomes were completed by Alfred Sturtevant.

Model Organism in Genetics

Drosophila is being extensively used in biological research, particularly for genetical, cellular, molecular, developmental and population studies. It has been used as model organism for research for almost a century. It has richly contributed to our understanding of pattern of inheritance, variation, mutation and speciation. Studies have also been made on the population genetics of different species of this genus. However most of these studies have been carried out in the laboratory by many workers. *D. melanogaster* types (clockwise): brown eyes with black body, cinnabar eyes, sepia eyes with ebony body, vermilion eyes, white eyes, and wild-type eyes with yellow body. *Drosophila melanogaster* is one of the most studied organisms in biological research, particularly in genetics and developmental biology. There are several reasons:

- The care and culture requires little equipment and use little space even when using large cultures with low cost. It is small and easy to grow in the laboratory and their morphology is easy to identify once they are anesthetized (usually with ether, carbon dioxide gas, by cooling them, or with products like FlyNap)
- Males do not show meiotic recombination, facilitating genetic studies.
- *Drosophila* has a short generation time (about 10 days at room temperature) so several generations can be studied within a few weeks.
- It has a high fecundity (females lay up to 100 eggs per day, and perhaps 2000 in a lifetime).
- Males and females are readily distinguished and virgin females are easily isolated, facilitating genetic crossing.
- The mature larvae show giant chromosomes in the salivary glands called polytene chromosomes— "puffs" indicate regions of transcription and hence gene activity.
- It has only four pairs of chromosomes: three autosomes, and one sex chromosome.

- Recessive lethal "balancer chromosomes" carrying visible genetic markers can be used to keep stocks of lethal alleles in a heterozygous state without recombination due to multiple inversions in the balancer.
- Genetic transformation techniques have been available since 1987.
- Its complete genome was sequenced and first published in 2000.

Genetic Markers

Genetic markers are commonly used in *Drosophila* research, for example within balancer chromosomes or P-element inserts, and most phenotypes are easily identifiable either with the naked eye or under a microscope. In the list of example common markers below, the allele symbol is followed by the name of the gene affected and a description of its phenotype.

(Note: *Recessive alleles are in lower case, while dominant alleles are capitalised.*)

- Cy^1: curly; the wings curve away from the body, flight may be somewhat impaired.
- e^1: ebony; Black body and wings (heterozygotes are also visibly darker than wild type).
- Sb^1: stubble; Hairs are shorter and thicker than wild type.
- w^1: white; Eyes lack pigmentation and appear white, vision may be somewhat impaired.
- y^1: yellow; Body pigmentation and wings appear yellow.

Drosophila genes are traditionally named after the phenotype they cause when mutated. For example, the absence of a particular gene in *Drosophila* will result in a mutant embryo that does not develop a heart. Scientists have thus called this gene tinman, named after the Oz character of the same name. This system of nomenclature results in a wider range of gene names than in other organisms.

Chromosome of Drosophila

D. melanogaster chromosomes to scale with megabase-pair references oriented as in the National Center for Biotechnology Information database. Centimorgan distances are approximate and estimated from the locations of selected mapped loci. The genome of *D. melanogaster* (sequenced in 2000, and curated at the FlyBase database contains four pairs of chromosomes: an X/Y pair, and three autosomes labeled 2, 3, and 4. The fourth chromosome is so tiny that it is often ignored, aside from its important eyeless gene. The *D. melanogaster* sequenced genome of 165 million base pairs has been annotated and contains approximately 13,767 protein-coding genes which comprise ~20% of the genome out of a total of an estimated 14,000 genes. More than 60% of the genome appears to be functional non-protein-coding DNA involved in gene expression control. Determination of sex in *Drosophila* occurs by the ratio of X chromosomes to autosomes, not because of the presence of a Y chromosome as in human sex determination. Although the Y chromosome is entirely heterochromatic, it contains at least 16 genes, many of which are thought to have male-related functions. About 75 per cent of known human disease genes have a recognizable match in the genetic code of fruit flies, and 50 per cent of fly protein sequences have mammalian homologs. An online database called Homophila is available to search for human disease gene homologues in flies and vice versa. *Drosophila* is being used as a genetic model for several human diseases including the neurodegenerative disorders Parkinson's, Huntington's, spinocerebellar ataxia and Alzheimer's disease. The fly is also being used to study mechanisms underlying aging and oxidative stress, immunity, diabetes, and cancer, as well as drug abuse.

Development of Fruit Fly

Development in *Drosophila* has been extensively studied, as its small size, short generation time, and large brood size makes it ideal for genetic studies. It is also unique among model organisms in that cleavage occurs in a syncytium. *Drosophila melanogaster*: During oogenesis, cytoplasmic bridges called "ring canals" connect the forming oocyte to nurse cells. Nutrients and developmental control molecules move from the nurse cells into the oocyte. In the figure to the left, the forming oocyte can be seen to be covered by follicular support cells. After fertilization of the oocyte the early embryo (or syncytial embryo) undergoes rapid DNA replication and 13 nuclear divisions until approximately 5000 to 6000 nuclei accumulate in the unseparated cytoplasm of the embryo. By the end of the 8th division most nuclei have migrated to the surface, surrounding the yolk sac (leaving behind only a few nuclei, which will become the yolk nuclei). After the 10th division the pole cells form at the posterior end of the embryo, segregating the germ line from the syncytium. Finally, after the 13th division cell membranes slowly invaginate, dividing the syncytium into individual somatic cells. Once this process is completed gastrulation starts. Nuclear division in the early *Drosophila* embryo happens so quickly there are no proper checkpoints so mistakes may be made in division of the DNA. To get around this problem the nuclei which have made a mistake detach from their centrosomes and fall into the centre of the embryo (yolk sac) which will not form part of the fly. The gene network (transcriptional and protein interactions) governing the early development of the fruit fly embryo is one of the best understood gene networks to date, especially the patterning along the antero-posterior (AP) and Dorso-ventral (DV) axes. The embryo undergoes well-characterized morphogenetic movements during gastrulation and early development, including germ-band extension, formation of several furrows, ventral invagination of the mesoderm, posterior and anterior invagination of endoderm (gut), as well as extensive body segmentation until finally hatching from the surrounding cuticle into a 1st-instar larva.

During larval development, tissues known as imaginal discs grow inside the larva. Imaginal discs develop to form most structures of the adult body, such as the head, legs, wings, thorax and genitalia. Cells of the imaginal disks are set aside during embryogenesis and continue to grow and divide during the larval stages - unlike most other cells of the larva which have differentiated to perform specialized functions and grow without further cell division. At metamorphosis, the larva forms a pupa, inside which the larval tissues are reabsorbed and the imaginal tissues undergo extensive morphogenetic movements to form adult structures.

Immunity

The *D. melanogaster* immune system can be divided into two responses: humoral and cell-mediated. The former is a systemic response mediated through the Toll and imd pathways, which are parallel systems for detecting microbes. *D. melanogaste*r has a "fat body" which is thought to be homologous to the human liver. It is the primary secretory organ and produces antimicrobial peptides. These peptides are secreted into the hemolymph and bind infectious bacteria, killing them by forming pores in their cell walls. Years ago many drug companies wanted to purify these peptides and use them as antibiotics.

Behavioural Genetics and Neuroscience

In 1971, Ron Konopka and Seymour Benzer published "Clock mutants of *Drosophila melanogaster*", a paper describing the first mutations that affected an animal's behavior. Wild-type flies show an activity rhythm with a frequency of about a day (24 hours). They found mutants with faster and slower rhythms as well as broken rhythms-flies that move and rest in random spurts. Work over the following 30 years has shown that these mutations (and others like them) affect a group of genes and their products that comprise a biochemical or biological clock. This clock is found in a wide range of fly cells, but the clock-bearing cells that control activity are several dozen neurons in the fly's central brain. Since then, Benzer and others have used behavioral screens to isolate genes involved in vision, olfaction, audition, learning/memory, courtship, pain and other processes, such as longevity. The first learning and memory mutants (*dunce, rutabaga* etc.) were isolated by William "Chip" Quinn while in Benzer's lab, and were eventually shown to encode components of an intracellular signaling pathway involving cyclic AMP, protein kinase A and a transcription factor known as CREB. These molecules were shown to be also involved in synaptic plasticity in *Aplysia* and mammals. Male flies sing to the females during courtship using their wing to generate sound, and some of the genetics of sexual behavior have been characterized. In particular, the fruitless gene has several different splice forms, and male flies expressing female splice forms have female-like behaviour and vice-versa.

Furthermore, *Drosophila* has been used in neuropharmacological research, including studies of cocaine and alcohol consumption. Sexual behaviour of Drosophila is very peculiar. One can observe sexual behavior by choosing a virgin female and bachelor male and introduce into an Elens-Wattiaux mating chamber (5 cm × 5 cm circular glass chamber with a lid to facilitate easy observation). Usually maximum mating occurs during morning hours, observation can be done between 7 and 11 a.m. Sexual behavioral acts such as courtship latency (time between introduction of male and female together into mating chamber and orientation of male towards female), mating latency (time between introduction of males and females into mating chamber and initiation of copulation of each pair), copulation duration (time between initiation and termination of copulation of each pair) were recorded. The quantitative behavioral acts of males such as tapping where male is going to tap the female one with help of the foreleg, circling is the phenomenon where the bachelor male is going to take a circle around the female, vibration where male is going to vibrate its wing court ship activities, licking is sexual behaviour exhibited by male where it is going to lick the female genetial operature. and female quantitative sexual behavior such as extruding, decamping and ignoring can also be recorded.

Vision

The compound eye of the fruit fly contains 760 unit eyes or ommatidia, and are one of the most advanced among insects. Each ommatidium contains 8 photoreceptor cells (R1-8), support cells, pigment cells, and a cornea. Wild-type flies have reddish pigment cells, which serve to absorb excess blue light so the fly isn't blinded by ambient light. Each photoreceptor cell consists of two main sections, the cell body and the rhabdomere. The cell body contains the nucleus while the 100-µm-long rhabdomere is made up of toothbrush-like stacks of membrane called microvilli. Each microvillus is 1-2 µm in length and ~60 nm in diameter. The membrane of the rhabdomere is packed with about 100 million rhodopsin molecules, the visual protein that absorbs light. The rest of the visual proteins are also tightly packed into the microvillar space, leaving little room for cytoplasm. The photoreceptors in *Drosophila* express a variety of rhodopsin isoforms. The R1-R6 photoreceptor cells express Rhodopsin1 (Rh1) which absorbs blue light (480 nm). The R7 and R8 cells express a combination of either Rh3 or Rh4 which absorb UV light (345 nm and 375 nm), and Rh5 or Rh6 which absorb blue (437 nm) and green (508 nm) light respectively. Each rhodopsin molecule consists of an opsin protein covalently linked to a carotenoid chromophore, 11-cis-3-hydroxyretinal.

As in vertebrate vision, visual transduction in invertebrates occurs via a G protein-coupled pathway. However, in vertebrates the G protein is transducin, while the G protein in invertebrates is Gq (dgq in *Drosophila*). When rhodopsin (Rh) absorbs a photon of light its chromophore, 11-cis-3-hydroxyretinal, is isomerized to all-trans-3-hydroxyretinal. Rh undergoes a conformational change into its active form, metarhodopsin. Metarhodopsin activates Gq, which in turn activates a phospholipase Cβ (PLCβ) known as NorpA.

PLCβ hydrolyzes phosphatidylinositol (4,5)-bisphosphate (PIP_2), a phospholipid found in the cell membrane, into soluble inositol triphosphate (IP_3) and diacylgycerol (DAG), which stays in the cell membrane. DAG or a derivative of DAG causes a calcium selective ion channel known as TRP (transient receptor potential) to open and calcium and sodium flows into the cell. IP_3 is thought to bind to IP3 receptors in the subrhabdomeric cisternae, an extension of the endoplasmic reticulum, and cause release of calcium, but this process doesn't seem to be essential for normal vision. Calcium binds to proteins such as calmodulin (CaM) and an eye-specific protein kinase C (PKC) known as InaC. These proteins interact with other proteins and have been shown to be necessary for shut off of the light response. In addition, proteins called arrestins bind metarhodopsin and prevent it from activating more Gq. A sodium-calcium exchanger known as CalX pumps the calcium out of the cell. It uses the inward sodium gradient to export calcium at a stoichiometry of 3 Na^+/1 Ca^{++}.[25] TRP, InaC, and PLC form a signaling complex by binding a scaffolding protein called InaD. InaD contains five binding domains called PDZ domain proteins which specifically bind the C termini of target proteins. Disruption of the complex by mutations in either the PDZ domains or the target proteins reduces the efficiency of signaling. For example, disruption of the interaction between InaC, the protein kinase C, and InaD results in a delay in inactivation of the light response. Unlike vertebrate metarhodopsin, invertebrate metarhodopsin can be converted back into rhodopsin by absorbing a photon of orange light (580 nm). Approximately two-thirds of the Drosophila brain is dedicated to visual processing. Although the spatial resolution of their vision is significantly worse than that of humans, their temporal resolution is approximately ten times better.

Flight

The wings of a fly are capable of beating at up to 220 times per second. Flies fly via straight sequences of movement interspersed by rapid turns called saccades. During these turns, a fly is able to rotate 90 degrees in fewer than 50 milliseconds. It was long thought that the characteristics of *Drosophila* flight were dominated by the viscosity of the air, rather than the inertia of the fly body. However, research in the lab of Michael Dickinson has indicated that flies perform banked turns, where the fly accelerates, slows down while turning, and accelerates again at the end of the turn. This indicates that inertia is the dominant force, as is the case with larger flying animals. Recent work, however, has shown that while the viscous effects on the insect body during flight may be negligible, the aerodynamic forces on the wings themselves actually cause fruit flies' turns to be damped viscously.

3 Ants

Ants occupy a wide range of ecological niches, and are able to exploit a wide range of food resources either as direct or indirect herbivores, predators and scavengers. Most species are omnivorous generalists but a few are specialist feeders. Their ecological dominance may be measured by their biomass, and estimates in different environments suggest that they contribute 15-20% (on average and nearly 25% in the tropics) of the total terrestrial animal biomass, which exceeds that of the vertebrates. Ants range in size from 0.75 to 52 millimeters (0.030-2.0 in), and vary in colour. Most ants are red or black, but a few species are green and some tropical species have a metallic luster. Ants are aiming the most prevalent pests in households. They are also found in restaurants, hospitals, offices, warehouses and other buildings where they can find food and water. On outdoor (and sometimes indoor) plants, ants protect and care for honeydew-producing insects such as aphid's soft scales, whiteflies, and mealy bugs, increasing damage from these pests. Ants also perform many useful functions in the environment, such as feeding on other pests. (eg: fleas, caterpillar, termites), dead insects and decomposing tissue from dead animals.

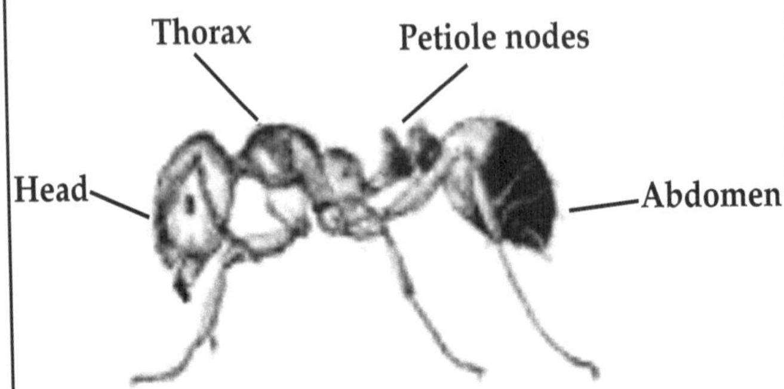

Ants and Body Parts

There are over 11000 species of ants through out the world. In India there are about 200 species, but fewer that a dozen are important pests. The most common ant occurring in and around the house and garden found example in Mysore is the argentine ant, Linepithema humile. Other common ant pests include the pharaoh ant (*monomorium pharaonis*), the odourous house ant (*Tapinoma sessile*).The thief ant (*Solenopsis molesta*), and the southern fire ant (Solenopsis xyloni). The velvety tree ant Liometopum occidentale, nests in old wood and is common outdoor species in landscapes.

Ants are distinct in their morphology from other insects in having elbowed antennae, metapleural glands, and a strong constriction of their second abdominal segment into a node-like petiole. The head, mesosoma and metasoma or gaster are the three distinct body segments. The petiole forms a narrow waist between their mesosoma (thorax plus the first abdominal segment, which is fused to it) and gaster (abdomen less the abdominal segments in the petiole). The petiole can be formed by one or two nodes (the second alone, or the second and third abdominal segments).

Like other insects, ants have an exoskeleton, an external covering that provides a protective casing around the body and a point of attachment for muscles, in contrast to the internal skeletons of humans and other vertebrates. Insects do not have lungs; oxygen and other gases like carbon dioxide pass through their exoskeleton through tiny valves called spiracles. Insects also lack closed blood vessels; instead, they have a long, thin, perforated tube along the top of the body (called the "dorsal aorta") that functions like a heart, and pumps haemolymph towards the head, thus driving the circulation of the internal fluids. The nervous system consists of a ventral nerve cord that runs the length of the body, with several ganglia and branches along the way reaching into the extremities of the appendages.

Key to Identifying Common Household Ants

Ants belong to the insects order Hymenoptera and these are close relatives of bees and wasps. They are familiar insects that are easily recognized, especially in their common wingless adult forms, known as workers. However winged forms of ants which leave the nest in large number in arm weather to mate and establish new colonies are often mistaken for winged termites, which also leave their nests to mate. Ants and termites can be distinguished by three main characteristics:

- Winged female and worker ants have antennae; the termite's antennae are not elbowed and different.
- The ant's body is constricted giving it the appearance of having a thin waist; the termite's body is not constricted.
- The ant's hind wings are smaller than fore wings; the termite's front and hind wings are about the same size. (shortly after their flights, both ants and termites lose their wings , some wings may not always be present).

Ants undergo complete metamorphosis, passing through egg, larval, pupal and adult stages. Larvae are immobile and wormlike and do not resemble adults. Ants are social insects with duties divided among different types, of adult individuals. Queen used to conduct the reproductive functions of a colony and is larger than other ants; they lay eggs and sometimes participate in the feeding and grooming of larvae. Female workers, who are sterile, gather food feed and care for the larvae build tunnels and defends the colony; these workers make up the bulk of the colony. Males do not participate in colony activities; their sole purpose is to mate with the queens. Few numbers of males are fed and cared for but workers. Basically the ants are two types depending on the nodes 1. One node ant and two nodes ant.

Carpenter Ants

C. pennsylvanicus can be distinguished from other carpenter ant species by the dull black colour of the head and body, and by whitish or yellowish hairs on the abdomen. All castes of this species (including the major and minor workers, queens, and males) are black or blackish. Colonies have workers that are not all the same size (polymorphism). The antennae are elbowed, usually with 6-13 segments. Workers on average range from 1-2 cm long. *C.vicinus* they possess only one bulge at their narrow "waist" (the single node on their petiole) and an evenly rounded back, when viewed from the side (known as a smooth dorsal thoracic profile). These ants are common in India. *C. clarithorax*, which are smaller they are found in the yellow and black these species are common in California, ranges from a little longer than 1/8 of an inch to not quite 5/16 of an inch long. *C. vicinus* varies in colour but usually is black and red. A smaller, yellow and black species, Carpenter ant can't sting but inflict painful bites with their powerful jaws and spray formic acid into the wound, causing a burning sensation.

Carpenter ants Large, 1/4 to 1/2 Inch, Black or Bicoloured Red or Black

One Node Ant and Two Nodes Ant

Example for the one node is carpenter ants and carpenter ants usually like sweets. They live in tree stumps,firewood, fence posts, hollow doors or window frames; deposit sawdust like frass outside of nests. People confuse the winged males and females that leave the nest on mating flights with termites. However, you can distinguish between ants and termites by the differences in their antennae, waist and wings. Also, carpenter ant sawdust is fibrous versus the 6-sided shaped pellets of dry wood termites. Argentine ant are commonly found in outdoors in shallow mounds usually they like foods such as sweets. They are 1/8 inch, dull brown.

Odorous House Ant

Argentine Ant

This ant belongs to group Tapinoma sessile these like sometimes proteins and sweets, and going to be nest in shallow mounds in soil or debris, or indoors in wall voids, around water pipes or heaters. The size of these group is around 1/8 inch, dark brown to shiny black; very strong odor when crushed.

Velvety tree ant (*Liometopum occidentale*) the food of these ant are sweets and insects. in dead wood such as old tree limbs, stumps, and logs. These are about 1/8 to 1/4 inch, brownish-black head, red thorax, and velvety black abdomen; they are produce distinct odor when crushed.

House Ant

Velvety Tree Ant

Two Lobed Ant

Pavement ant (*Tetra-morium caespitum*) these are the ant which have two lobes.Proteins, sweets, and even a kind of grease are kind of food preferred by this type of ant. These are commonly nest in the lawns or under stones, boards build mounds along sidewalks, foundation, and near water. These are about 3/16 inch, colour are around dark brown to black.

Pavement Ant

Red imported fire ant (*Solenopsis invicta*) these are the ant which are reddish with dark brown abdomen in look and measure about 1/16 to 1/5 inch. It takes sweets, proteins.

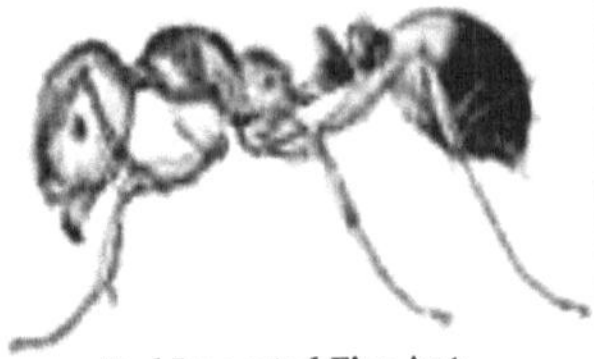

Red Imported Fire Ant

These built their nest in mounds with multiple openings in soil or lawns and sometimes in buildings behind wall voids.

Southern Fire Ant

Southern fire ant (*Solenopsis xyloni*) these are going to measure around 1/8 to 1/4 inch. The abdomen is black, amber head and thorax and body is covered by the brown hairs. The composition of their food is proteins and sweets. They are found under the woods and rocks.

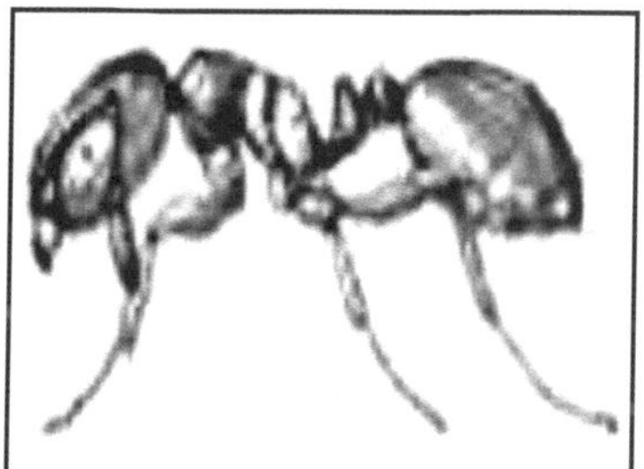

Thief Ant

Thief ant (*Solenopsis molesta*) these are the ants commonly found in the indoors behind wallboards or base-boards or outdoors in soil, under rocks or decaying wood. These ants like greasy and fatty foods, sometimes sweets. The most important character of this ant is stealing food and ant larvae from other ant nests. They are yellow and reddish in colour.

Colony Dynamics and Life Cycle

Carpenter ants feed on dead and living insects, nectar, fruit juices and sugary honeydew excreted by plant sucking insects. They will enter buildings in search of nesting sites or moisture and can build nests containing several buildings in search of nestings sites or moisture and can build nests containing several thousands ants. Typically, the nests they construct indoors are satellites of a larger, parent nest located outside in a live or dead tree, a woodpile, or landscaping materials. Several satellite nests can be associated with a single parent nest, where the queens resides in the case of *C. vicinus*, which can have as many as 40 queens in a single nest. Ants undergo complete metamorphosis, passing through egg, larval, pupal and adult stages. Larvae are immobile and wormlike and do not resemble adults. New reproductive one has wings and leaves the nest on mating flights in the spring. The timing of these flights varies for each species. For example, *C. modoc* swarms in the late afternoon, often a heavy rainfall. After the mating flight, males die and inseminated queens disperse in search of potential nest sites such as dead tree or stump. Here, the newly mated queen excavates a chamber, seals herself in and begins laying eggs. There colony growth is slow at first and only after several years does the colony reach maturity and begin producing a new generation of winged ants to begin the cycle again. The life of an ant starts from an egg. If the egg is fertilized, the progeny will be female (diploid); if not, it will be male (haploid). Ants develop by complete metamorphosis with the larval stages passing through a pupal stage before emerging as an adult. The larva is largely immobile and is fed and cared for by workers. Food is given to the larvae by trophallaxis, a process in which an ant regurgitates liquid food held in its crop. This is also how adults share food, stored in the "social stomach", among them. Larvae may also be provided with solid food such as tropic eggs, pieces of prey and seeds brought back by foraging workers and may even be transported directly to captured prey in some species.

The larvae grow through a series of moults and enter the pupal stage. The pupa has the appendages free and not fused to the body as in a butterfly pupa. The differentiation into queens and workers (which are both female), and different castes of workers (when they exist), is determined by the nutrition the larvae obtain. Larvae and pupae need to be kept at fairly constant temperatures to ensure proper development, and so are often moved around the various brood chambers within the colony. A new worker spends the first few days of its adult life caring for the queen and young. It then graduates to digging and other nest work, and later to defending the nest and foraging. These changes are sometimes fairly sudden, and define what are called temporal castes. An explanation for the sequence is suggested by the high casualties involved in foraging, making it an acceptable risk only for ants that are older and are likely to die soon of natural causes. Ants usually nest in soil; nest sites vary with species but are often found next to buildings, along side walks, or in close proximity to food sources such as trees or plants that harbor honeydew producing insects. They also construct nests under boards, stones, tree stumps or plants and sometimes under buildings or other protected places. In temperate climates the pharoh ant nests indoors preferring warm mist locations often in voids, under flooring, or near hot water pipes or heating systems but is also found nesting outdoors in warmer parts of any country. Ant foods include fruit, seeds, nuts, fatty substances, dead or live insect's dead animals and sweets. Food preferences vary among ant species. Ants often enter buildings seeking food and water, warmth and shelter or a refuge from dry hot weather or flooded conditions. They may appear suddenly in buildings if other food sources become unavailable or weather conditions change.

A new colony is typically established by a single newly mated queen. After weeks or moths of confinement underground, she lays her first egg. After the eggs hatch , she feeds the white, legless larvae with her own metabolized wing muscles and fat bodies until they pupate. Several weeks later the pupae transform into sterile female adult workers and the first workers dig their way out of the nest to collect food for themselves for the queen (who continues to lay eggs) and for subsequent broods of larvae. After a few years, the colony begins to produce winged male and female ants, which leave the nest to mate and form new colonies.

TYPICAL ANT LIFE CYCLE

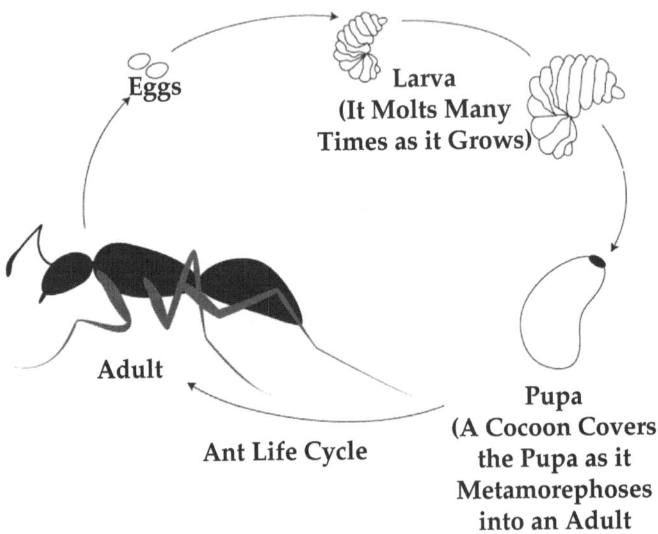

Ant Life Cycle

In the colonies of a few ant species, there are physical castes discrimination-workers in distinct size-classes, called minor, median, and major workers. Often the larger ants have disproportionately larger heads, and correspondingly stronger mandibles. Such individuals are sometimes called "soldier" ants because their stronger mandibles make them more effective in fighting, although they are still workers and their "duties" typically do not vary greatly from the minor or median workers. In a few species the median workers are absent, creating a sharp divide between the minors and majors. Weaver ants, for example, have a distinct bimodal size distribution. Some other species show continuous variation in the size of workers. The smallest and largest workers in *Pheidologeton diversus* show nearly a 500-fold difference in their dry-weights. Workers cannot mate; however, because of the haplodiploid sex-determination system in ants, workers of a number of species can lay unfertilised eggs that become fully fertile haploid males. The role of workers may change with their age and in some species, such as honeypot ants, young workers are fed until their gasters are distended, and act as living food storage vessels. These food storage workers are called *repletes*. This polymorphism in morphology and behaviour of workers was initially thought to be determined by environmental factors such as nutrition and hormones which led to different developmental paths; however, genetic differences between worker castes have been noted in *Acromyrmex* sp. These polymorphisms are caused by relatively small genetic changes; differences in a single gene of *Solenopsis invicta* can decide whether the colony will have single or multiple queens. The Australian jack jumper ant (*Myrmecia pilosula*), has only a single pair of chromosomes (males have just one chromosome as they are haploid), the lowest number known for any animal, making it an interesting subject for studies in the genetics and developmental biology of social insects.

There are some ants which are called weaver ants collaborating to dismember a red ant (the two at the extremities are pulling the red ant, while the middle one cuts the red ant until it snaps). Ants communicate with each other using pheromones. These chemical signals are more developed in ants than in other hymenopteran groups. Like other insects, ants perceive smells with their long, thin and mobile antennae. The paired antennae provide information about the direction and intensity of scents. Since most ants live on the ground, they use the soil surface to leave pheromone trails that can be followed by other ants. In species that forage in groups, a forager that finds food marks a trail on the way back to the colony; this trail is followed by other ants, these ants then reinforce the trail when they head back with food to the colony. When the food source is exhausted, no new trails are marked by returning ants and the scent slowly dissipates. This behaviour helps ants deal with changes in their environment. For instance, when an established path to a food source is blocked by an obstacle, the foragers leave the path to explore new routes. If an ant is successful, it leaves a new trail marking the shortest route on its return. Successful trails are followed by more ants, reinforcing better routes and gradually finding the best path.

Ants use pheromones for more than just making trails. A crushed ant emits an alarm pheromone that sends nearby ants into attack frenzy and attracts more ants from further away. Several ant species even use "propaganda pheromones" to confuse enemy ants and make them fight among themselves. Pheromones are produced by a wide range of structures including Dufour's glands, poison glands and glands on the hindgut, pygidium, rectum, sternum and hind tibia. Pheromones are also exchanged mixed with food and passed by trophallaxis, transferring information within the colony. This allows other ants to detect what task group (e.g., foraging or nest maintenance) other colony members belong to. In ant species with queen castes, workers begin to raise new queens in the colony when the dominant queen stops producing a specific pheromone.

Learning

Many animals can learn behaviour by imitation but ants may be the only group apart from mammals where interactive teaching has been observed. A knowledgeable forager of *Temnothorax albipennis* leads a naive nest-mate to newly discovered food by the process of tandem running. The follower obtains knowledge through its leading tutor. Both leader and follower are acutely sensitive to the progress of their partner with the leader slowing down when the follower lags, and speeding up when the follower gets too close.

Controlled experiments with colonies of *Cerapachys biroi* suggest that individuals may choose nest roles based on their previous experience. An entire generation of identical workers was divided into two groups whose outcome in food foraging was controlled. One group was continually rewarded with prey, while it was made certain that the other failed. As a result, members of the successful group intensified their foraging attempts while the unsuccessful group ventured out less and less. A month later, the successful foragers continued in their role while the others moved to specialize in brood care.

Construction of the Colony

Leaf nest of Ants: usually ants nest on trees and form subterranean nests Complex nests are built by many ants, but other species are nomadic and do not build permanent structures. There are the cases of the nest formation on the ground, under stones or logs, inside logs and hollow stems or even acorns. The materials used for construction include soil and plant matter. Ants carefully select their nest sites; some species like *Temnothorax albipennis* will avoid sites with dead ants, as these may indicate the presence of pests or disease. They are quick to abandon established nests at the first sign of threats.

In South Africa and America, there are ants which are called army ants. The army ants of South America and the driver ants of Africa do not build permanent nests, but instead alternate between nomadism and stages where the workers form a temporary nest from their own bodies, by holding each other together. In case of weaver ant wokers nest in tress by attaching leaves together, first pulling them together with bridges of workers and then inducing their larvae to produce silk as they are moved along the leaf edges. Similar forms of nest construction are seen in some species of *Polyrhachis*.

Navigation

Usually ants travel distances of up to 200-250 meters (800 ft) from their nest and usually find their way back using scent trails. Some ants forage at night. Day foraging ants in hot and arid regions face death by desiccation, so the ability to find the shortest route back to the nest reduces that risk. Several species of ants are able to use the Earth's magnetic field. Ants have compound eyes have specialized cells that detect polarized light from the Sun, which is used to determine direction. These polarization detectors are sensitive in the ultraviolet region of the light spectrum. Diurnal desert ants such as *Cataglyphis fortis* use visual landmarks in combination with other cues to navigate. In the absence of visual landmarks, the closely related Sahara desert ant such as *Cataglyphis bicolour* navigates by keeping track of direction as well as distance travelled, like an internal pedometer that counts how many steps they take in each direction. They integrate this information to find the shortest route back to their nest. In some army ant species, a group of foragers that get separated from the main column can sometimes turn back on themselves and form a circular ant mill. The workers may then run around continuously until they die of exhaustion.

Locomotion

Reproductive females lose their wings after their mating flights in order to begin their colonies and worker ants do not have wings. Therefore, unlike their wasp ancestors, most ants travel by walking. Some species are capable of leaping. For example, *Harpegnathos saltator* which is commonly Jerdon's jumping ant is able to jump by synchronising the action of its mid and hind pairs of legs. There are several species of gliding ant including *Cephalotes atratus*, this may be a common character among most arboreal ants. Ants with this ability are able to control the direction of their descent while falling. Some species of ants can form chains to bridge gaps over water, underground, or through spaces in vegetation. Some species also form floating rafts that help them survive floods. These rafts may also have a role in allowing ants to colonize islands.

Polyrhachis sokolova, a species of ant found in Australian mangrove swamps, can swim and live in underwater nests. Since they lack gills, they breathe in trapped pockets of air in the submerged nests.

Collection of the Food

In most case ants are generalist scavengers, predators and indirect herbivores but a few have evolved specialized ways of obtaining nutrition. *Atta* and *Acromyrmex* called Leafcutter ants feed exclusively on a fungus that grows only within their colonies. They continually collect leaves which are taken to the colony, cut into tiny pieces and placed in fungal gardens. Workers specialize in tasks according to their sizes. The largest ants cut stalks, smaller workers chew the leaves and the smallest tend the fungus. Leafcutter ants are sensitive enough to recognize the reaction of the fungus to different plant material, apparently detecting chemical signals from the fungus. If a particular type of leaf is toxic to the fungus the colony will no longer collect it. The ants feed on structures produced by the fungi called *gongylidia*. Symbiotic bacteria on the exterior surface of the ants produce antibiotics that kill bacteria that may harm the fungi. Honey pot ants, store food to prevent colony famine.

Some species such as Tetramorium caespitum attack and take over neighboring ant colonies. Others are fewer expansionists but just as aggressive; they invade colonies to steal larvae or eggs and also food, which thcy cither eat or raise as workers/slaves. Extreme specialists among these slave-raiding ants, such as the Amazon ants, are incapable of feeding themselves and need captured workers to survive. Captured workers of the enslaved species Temnothorax have evolved a counter strategy, destroying just the female pupae of the slave-making Protomognathus americanus, but sparing the males (who don't take part in slave-raiding as adults). Meat-eater ants feeding on a cicada. Social ants cooperate and collectively gather food. Not all ants have the same kind of societies. The Australian bulldog ants are among the biggest and most basal (primitive) of ants. Each individual ants hunts alone, using its large eyes instead of its chemical senses to find prey. There are the cases where there is a worker *Harpegnathos saltator* species of the ants are going to battle with their queen. Ants identify kin and nestmates through their scent, which comes from hydrocarbon-laced secretions that coat their exoskeletons. If an ant is separated from its original colony, it will eventually lose the colony scent. Any ant that enters a colony without a matching scent will be attacked.

Parasitic ant species enter the colonies of host ants and establish themselves as social parasites; species like *Strumigenys xenos* are entirely parasitic and do not have workers, but instead rely on the food gathered by their *Strumigenys perplexa* hosts. This form of parasitism is seen across many ant genera, but the parasitic ant is usually a species that is closely related to its host. A variety of methods are employed to enter the nest of the host ant. A parasitic queen can enter the host nest before the first brood has hatched, establishing herself prior to development of a colony scent. Other species use pheromones to confuse the host ants or to trick them into carrying the parasitic queen into the nest. Some simply fight their way into the nest. Fungus-growing ants that make up the tribe Attini, including leafcutter ants, cultivate certain species of fungus in the *Leucoagaricus* or *Leucocoprinus* genera of the Agaricaceae family. In this ant-fungus mutualism, both species depend on each other for survival. The ant *Allomerus decemarticulatus* has evolved a three-way association with the host plant *Hirtella physophora* (Chrysobalanaceae), and a sticky fungus which is used to trap their insect prey.

There are the reports by some experts regarding conflict between the sexes of a species is seen in some species of ants with the reproductive apparently competing to produce offspring that are as closely related to them as possible. The most extreme form involves the production of clonal offspring. An extreme of sexual conflict is seen in *Wasmannia auropunctata*, where the queens produce diploid daughters by parthenogenesis and males produce clones by a process where a diploid egg loses its maternal contribution to produce haploid males that are clones of the father.

Relationships with Other Animals

According to researchers there are army ants which are notorious for "raids", in which huge numbers of ants forage simultaneously over a certain area, attacking prey Armies of as many as 2,500,000 such ants destroy almost all animal life they encounter. *Dorylus* species known as *Siafu*, attack everything in their path, including human beings. *Eciton burchellii* is the swarming ant most commonly attended by "ant-following" birds such as antbirds and woodcreepers. There are the case of symbiotic associations in ants with a range of species, including other ant species, other insects, plants, and fungi. They are preyed on by many animals and even certain fungi. Some arthropod species spend part of their lives within ant nests, preying on ants, their larvae and eggs, consuming the ants' food stores, or avoiding predators. These inquilines can bear a close resemblance to ants. The nature of this ant mimicry will varies, with some cases involving Batesian mimicry, where the mimic reduces the risk of predation.

Aphids and other hemipteran insects secrete sweet liquid called honeydew when they feed on plant sap. The sugars in honeydew are a high-energy food source, which many ant species collect. In some cases the aphids secrete the honeydew in response to the ants' tapping them with their antennae. The ants in turn keep predators away and will move the aphids between feeding locations. On migrating to a new area, many colonies will take the aphids with them, to ensure a continued supply of honeydew. Ants also tend mealybugs to harvest their honeydew. Mealybugs can become a serious pest of pineapples if ants are present to protect mealybugs from their natural enemies. Lemon ants make devil's gardens by killing surrounding plants with their stings and leaving a pure patch of lemon ant trees (*Duroia hirsuta*). This modification of the forest provides the ants with more nesting sites inside the stems of the *Duroia* trees. Some trees have extrafloral nectaries that provide food for ants, which in turn protect the plant from herbivorous insects. Species like the bullhorn acacia (Acacia cornigera) in Central America have hollow thorns that house colonies of stinging ants (*Pseudomyrmex ferruginea*) that defend the tree against insects, browsing mammals, and epiphytic vines. Isotopic labelling studies suggest that plants also obtain nitrogen from the ants. In return, the ants obtain food from protein and lipid rich Beltian bodies. Another example of this type of ectosymbiosis comes from the *Macaranga* tree, which has stems adapted to house colonies of *Crematogaster* ants. Many tropical tree species have seeds that are dispersed by ants. According to the research Seed dispersal by ants or the method of seed dispersal is called myrmecochory is widespread particularly in Africa and Australia. Some plants in fire-prone grassland systems are particularly dependent on ants for their survival and dispersal. Many ant-dispersed seeds have special external structures, elaiosomes,that are sought after by ants as food. A convergence, possibly a form of mimicry, is seen in the eggs of stick insects. They have an edible elaiosome-like structure and are taken into the ant nest where the young hatch.

In South Africa, ants are used to help harvest rooibos (*Aspalathus linearis*), which are small seeds used to make a herbal tea. The plant disperses its seeds widely, making manual collection difficult. Black ants collect and store these and other seeds in their nest, where humans can gather them en masse. Up to half a pound (200 g) of seeds can be collected from one ant-heap. Although most ants survive attempts by humans to eradicate them, a few are highly endangered. These are mainly island species that have evolved specialized traits and include the critically endangered Sri Lankan relict ant (*Aneuretus simoni*) and Adetomyrma venatrix of Madagascar.

Ants Used As Food

Today Ants and their larvae are eaten in different parts of the world. The eggs of two species of ants are the basis for the dish in some country known as *escamoles*. They are considered a form of insect caviar and can sell for as much as US $ 40 per pound (US $ 90/kg) because they are seasonal and hard to find. Acoording to the information from the web in Colombian department of Santander, *hormigas culonas* roughly and Atta laevigata are toasted alive and eaten. In areas of near India, and throughout Burma and Thailand, a paste of the green weaver ant (*Oecophylla smaragdina*) is served as a condiment with curry. Weaver ant eggs and larvae as well as the ants themselves may be used in a Thai salad, in a dish called *yum khai mod daeng* or red ant egg salad, a dish that comes from the Issan or north-eastern region of Thailand. Saville-Kent, in the *Naturalist in Australia* wrote "Beauty, in the case of the green ant, is more than skin-deep. Their attractive, almost sweetmeat-like translucency possibly invited the first essays at their consumption by the human species". Mashed up in water, after the manner of lemon squash, "these ants form a pleasant acid drink which is held in high favour by the natives of North Queensland, and is even appreciated by many European palates". According to reports given by my friend in some parts of Maland region of Karnataka there is a belief where there is improvement of eye sight by taking the ants as a food.

Ants As Pests

Pharaoh ant which is the small and tiny ant is a major pest in hospitals and office blocks and books self; it can make nests between sheets of paper. Some ant species are considered pests and because of the adaptive nature of ant colonies, eliminating the entire colony is nearly impossible. Pest management is therefore a matter of controlling local populations, instead of eliminating an entire colony, and most attempts at control are temporary solutions. Ants classified as pests include the pavement ant, yellow crazy ant, sugar ants, the Pharaoh ant, carpenter ants, Argentine ant, odorous house ants, red imported fire ant and European fire ant. Populations are controlled using insecticide baits, either in granule or liquid formulations. Bait is gathered by the ants as food and brought back to the nest where the poison is inadvertently spread to other colony members through trophallaxis. Boric acid and borax are often used as insecticides that are relatively safe for humans. Bait may be broadcast over a large area to control species like the red fire ant that occupy large areas. Nests of red fire ants may be destroyed by following the ants' trails back to the nest and then pouring boiling water into it to kill the queen. According to the information from the pest management this works in about 60% of the mounds and requires about 14 litres (3 imp gal; 4 US gal) per mound.

In Science and Technology

Myrmecologists it is a branch of ant science study about ants in the laboratory and in their natural conditions. Their complex and variable social structures have made ants ideal model organisms. Ultraviolet vision was first discovered in ants by Sir John Lubbok in 1881. Studies on ants have tested hypotheses in ecology, sociobiology and have been particularly important in examining the predictions of theories of kin selection and evolutionarily stable strategies. Ant colonies can be studied by rearing or temporarily maintaining them in formicaria, specially constructed glass framed enclosures. Individuals may be tracked for study by marking them with colours. The successful techniques used by ant colonies have been studied in computer science and robotics to produce distributed and fault-tolerant systems for solving problems. This area of biomimetics has led to studies of ant locomotion, search engines that make use of "foraging trails", fault-tolerant storage and networking algorithms.

Damage from the Ants

Carpenter ants don't consume wood like termites but excavate it to make their nest, which enlarge colonies can consist of an extensive network of galleries and tunnels often beginning in an area where there is damage from water or wood decay. From here they can expand the nest in wall voids, hollow doors, and insulation. Infestations can even occur in new buildings when land clearing in the surrounding area disturbs established colonies, causing them to move into the structure. In natural settings, they excavate into the heartwood of living trees or into dead trees and stumps. These latter infestations play an important role in the decomposition of wood. Inside buildings, household ants feed on sugars, syrups, honey fruit juice fats and meat. Long trails of thousand of ants may lead from nests to food source, causing considerable concern among building occupants. Outdoors they are attracted to honey dew, produced by soft scales, mealy bugs and aphids. This liquid excrement contains sugars and other nutrients. Frequently outbreaks of scales and aphids occur when ants tend them for honey dew because the ants protect scales and aphids from their natural enemies.

Ants can bite with their pincer like jaws although most species rarely do. The velvety tree ant, however is an aggressive bitter. A few ants sting, including native fire ants and harvester ants, which are primarily outdoor species and are the most common stinging ants in America. An aggressive stinging ant, the red imported fire ant (*S. invicta*), has recently been found in various southern California countries, if you suspect a fire ant infestation, report it to your country agricultural officer.

Management

There are several non chemical measures that can help prevent infestations:

- Trim tree branches and shrubs away from structures to prevent access;
- Seal off potential entry points such as where utility lines enter a structure;
- Reduce much around building perimeters to a depth of 2 to 3 inches to discourage nesting;
- Eliminate any earth-to-wood contact of structural elements that might promote wood decay;
- Replace decayed or damaged wood and correct problems that cause decay such as clogged rain gutters or leaky pipes;
- Increase ventilation to damp areas such as attic or sub floor spaces;
- Store firewood off the ground and several feet way from structures; and
- Remove potential food sources inside a structure and store them tightly sealed containers.

When numerous ants are found on plants, they are probably attracted to the sweet honeydew deposited on the plants by honeydew-producing insects such as aphids or soft scales. Ants may also be attracted up into trees or shrubs by ripening or rotten sweet fruit or floral nectar. These ants can be kept out by banding tree trunks with sticky substances such as Tanglefoot. Trim branches to keep them from touching structures or plants so that ants are forced to climb up the trunk to reach the foliage. Protect young or sensitive trees from possible injury by wrapping the trunk with a collar of heavy paper, duct tape, or fabric tree wrap and coating this with the sticky material. Check the sticky material every 1 or 2 weeks and stir it with a stick to prevent the material from getting clogged with debris and dead ants, which will allow ants to cross. Ant stakes with bait can also be used around trees. In landscapes, some mulches can repel ants and discourage nesting. For example, aromatic pencil cedar mulch repels Argentine ants, whereas pine straw provides an ideal nesting site. Be aware that not all types of cedar chips repel ants: the effectiveness of red cedar chips found in California has not been verified.

Baits are insecticides mixed with materials that attract worker ants looking for food. They are a key tool for managing ants and the only type of insecticide recommended in most situations. Ants are attracted to the bait and recruit other workers to it. Workers carry small portions of the bait back to the nest where it is transferred mouth-to-mouth to other workers, larvae, and queens and other reproductive forms to kill the entire colony. Bait products must be slow-acting so that the foraging ants have time to make their way back to the nest and feed other members of the colony before they are killed. When properly used, baits are more effective and safer than sprays there are the following methods to be used if there is a case of the ant emergency:

- Determine what the ants are attracted to and remove the food source.
- Vacuum trails, wipe them with soapy water, or spray with window cleaner.
- Locate entry points and caulk openings or plug with petroleum jelly.
- Put out bait stations or apply gel bait at entry points.
- Baits take time to work so continue to clean up trails.

Treatment Inside the House

If ants can be thoroughly washed away and excluded from an area, an insecticide is probably not necessary. Vacuuming up ant trails or sponging or mopping them with soapy water may be as effective as an insecticide spray in temporarily removing foraging ants in a building because it removes the ant's scent trail, especially if thorough cleaning is done at the entry points. Some soap products such as window cleaners can kill ants on contact but leave no residual toxicity. Certain plant-based oils are also applied for this purpose, but their odor can be offensive

Warning on the Use of Chemicals

Pesticides applied in your home and landscape can move and contaminate creeks, lakes and rivers. Confine chemicals to the property being treated and never allow them to get into drains or creeks. Avoid drift onto neighboring properties, especially gardens containing fruits or vegetables ready to be picked. Do not place containers containing pesticide in the trash or pour pesticides down sink, toilet, or out side drains. Either use the pesticide according to the label until the container is empty or take unwanted pesticides to a household hazardous waste collection site. Contact your agricultural officer for additional information on safe container disposal and for the location of the hazaradous waste collection site nearest you. Dispose of empty containers by following label direction. Never reuse or burn the container or dispose of them in such a manner that they contaminate water supplies or natural waterways. Pesticides (insecticide, herbicides and fungicides) are designed to be toxic to the pests they target. When used properly, pesticides can protect your plants or home from damage. However when the label instructions aren't followed accurately, plant injury can occur, pests might not be controlled, human health might be impaired, and pesticides can contribute to soil, air, or water pollution. Fertilizer products also can have negative environmental impacts when they get into waterways. Use pesticides only when non-chemical methods are ineffective and pests are reaching intolerable levels, and choose the least toxic most effective product.

4 Aphids

Aphids, also known as *plant lice* and these are also called as *greenflies* in Britain and commonwealth, *blackflies* or *whiteflies*, are small sap sucking insects, and belongs to members of the superfamily *Aphidoidea*. Aphids are small, soft bodied insects with long slender mouth parts that they use to pierce stems, leaves and other tender plant parts and suck out plant fluids. Almost every plant has one or more aphid species that occasionally feeds on it. Many aphid species are difficult to distinguish; however; identification to species is not necessary to control them in most situations. Aphids are among the most destructive insect pests on cultivated plants in temperate regions. The damage they do to plants has made them enemies of farmers and gardeners the world over, but from a zoological standpoint they are a very successful group of organisms. Aphids may be green, yellow, brown, and red or black depending on the species and the plants they feed on. A few species appear waxy or wooly due to the secretion of waxy white or gray substances over their body surface. All are small. Pear shaped insects with long legs and antennae. Most species have a pair of tube like structures called cornicles projecting backwards out of the hind end of their bodies. The presence of cornicles distinguishes aphids from all other insects.

There are about 5000 species of 10 families are known. Historically, many fewer families were recognized, as most species were included in the family Aphididae. Around 250 species are serious pests for agriculture and forestry as well as an annoyance for gardeners. They vary in length from one to ten millimetres. Natural enemies include predatory lady beetles (Coleoptera: Coccinellidae), hoverfly larvae (Diptera: Syrphidae), parasitic wasps, aphid midge larvae, crab spiders lacewings (Neuroptera: Chrysopidae), and entomopathogenic fungi like *Lecanicillium lecanii* and the Entomophthorales. Generally adult aphids are wingless, but most species also occur on winged forms, especially when populations are high or during spring and fall. The ability to produce winged individuals provides the pests with a way to disperse to other plants when the quality of the food source deteriorates. Although they may be found singly aphids often in dense groups on leaves or stems.Unlike leafhoppers, plant bugs and certain other insects that might be confused with them. Most aphids do not move rapidly when disturbed.

Food of Aphids

Many aphid species are feed on only one plant species. Others, like the green peach aphid (*Myzus persicae*), feed on hundreds of plant species. Aphids passively feed on sap of phloem vessels in plants, as do many of their fellow members of Hemiptera such as scale insects and cicadas. Once a phloem vessel is punctured, the sap, which is under high pressure, is forced into the aphid's food canal. Occasionally, aphids also ingest xylem sap, which is a more dilute diet than phloem sap as the concentration of sugars and amino acids are one per cent of those in the phloem. Xylem sap is under negative hydrostatic pressure and requires active sucking, suggesting an important role in aphid physiology. As xylem sap ingestion has been observed following a dehydration period, it was suspected that aphids consume xylem sap to replenish their water balance; the consumption of the dilute sap of xylem permitting aphids to rehydrate. However, recent data showed that aphids consume more xylem sap than expected and that they notably do so when they are not dehydrated and when their fecundity decreases. This suggests that aphids, and potentially, all the phloem-sap feeding species of the order Hemiptera, consume xylem sap for another reason than replenishing water balance. It was suggested that xylem sap consumption is related to osmoregulation.

Aphids are in the superfamily Aphidoidea in the homopterous division of the order Hemiptera. Recent classification within Hemiptera has reduced the old taxon "Homoptera" to two suborders: Sternorrhyncha (*e.g.*, aphids, whiteflies, scales, psyllids, etc.) and Auchenorrhyncha (e.g., cicadas, leafhoppers, treehoppers, planthoppers, etc.) with the suborder Heteroptera containing a large group of insects known as the true bugs. More recent reclassifications have substantially rearranged the families within Aphidoidea: some old families were reduced to subfamily rank (*e.g.* Eriosomatidae), and many old subfamilies elevated to family rank. Taxonomically woolly conifer aphids like the pine aphid, the spruce aphid and the balsam woolly aphid are not true aphids, but adelgids, and lack the cornicles of true aphids.

The damage can be assesses low to moderate numbers of leaf feeding aphids are usually not damaging in gardens or on trees, however, large populations cause curling, yellowing and distortion of leaves and stunting of shoots; they can also produce large quantities of a sticky exudates known as honeydew, which often turns black with the growth of a sooty mold fungus. Some aphid species inject a toxin into plants, which further distorts growth. A few species cause gall formation.

Aphids may transmit viruses from plant to plant certain vegetable and ornamental plants. Squashes, cucumbers, pumpkins, melons, Beans, potatoes, lettuces beets, chards and bok choy are crops that often have aphid transmitted viruses associated with them. The virus cause yellowing, mottling, or curling of leaves and stunting of plant growth. Although losses can be great, they are difficult to prevent through the control of aphids because infection occurs even aphid numbers are very low: it only takes a few minutes for the aphid to transmit the virus while it takes much longer time to kill the aphid with an insecticide. A few aphid species attack parts of plant other leaves and shoots. The lettuce root aphid is a soil dweller that attacks lettuce roots during most of its cycle, causing lettuce plants to wilt and occasionally die if populations are high. The lettuce root aphid over winters as eggs on poplar trees, where it produces leaf galls in spring and summer. The wooly apple aphid infests woody parts of apple roots and limbs, often near pruning wounds and can cause overall tree decline if roots are infested for several years.

Effect on Plants

Plants exhibiting aphid damage can have a variety of symptoms, such as decreased growth rates, mottled leaves, yellowing, stunted growth, curled leaves, browning, wilting, low yields and death. The removal of sap creates a lack of vigour in the plant, and aphid saliva is toxic to plants. Aphids frequently transmit disease-causing organisms like plant viruses to their hosts. The green peach aphid (*Myzus persicae*) is a vector for more than 110 plant viruses. Cotton aphids (*Aphis gossypii*) often infect sugarcane, papaya and groundnuts with viruses. Aphids contributed to the spread of late blight (*Phytophthora infestans*) among potatoes in the Great Irish Potato Famine of the 1840s. The cherry aphid or black cherry aphid, *Myzus cerasi*, is responsible for some leaf curl of cherry trees. This can easily be distinguished from 'leaf curl' caused by Taphrina fungus species due to the presence of aphids beneath the leaves. The coating of plants with honeydew can contribute to the spread of fungi which can damage plants. Honeydew produced by aphids has been observed to reduce the effectiveness of fungicides as well. A hypothesis that insect feeding may improve plant fitness was floated in the mid-1970s by Owen and Wiegert. It was felt that the excess honeydew would nourish soil micro-organisms, including nitrogen fixers. In a nitrogen poor environment, this could provide an advantage to an infested plant over a noninfested plant. However, this does not appear to be supported by the observational evidence. The damage of plants, and in particular commercial crops, has resulted in large amounts of resources and efforts being spent attempting to control the activities of aphids.

Management of the Aphids

Although aphids seldom kill a mature plant, the damage and unsightly honeydew they generate sometimes warrant control. Consider the non-chemical controls discussed below; most insecticides, if used will destroy beneficial insects along with the pest. On mature trees, such as in citrus orchards, aphids and the honeydew they produce can provide a valuable food source for beneficial insects. There are the reports where there aphids are very susceptible to fungal disease when it is humid. Whole colonies of aphids can be killed by these pathogens when conditions are right. Look for dead aphids that have turned reddish brown; they have a fuzzy, shriveled texture unlike the shiny, bloated, tan coloured mummies that form when aphids are parasitized. Weather can also impact aphids. Populations of many species are reduced by summer heat in the central valley a desert areas and aphids activity is also limited during the coldest part of the year. However, some aphids may be active year round, especially in the milder central coastal areas of Africa and India. There are various insecticides that can be used to control aphids. Nowadays, there are many plant extracts and plant products that are eco-friendly and control aphids as effectively as chemical insecticides. Researchers suggested use of Neem products and Lantana products to protect plants against aphids. Integrated pest management of various species of aphids can be achieved using biological insecticides based on microbes such as *Beauveria bassiana* or *Paecilomyces fumosoroseus*.

Biological Control

Natural enemies can be very important in the control of aphids, especially in gardens not sprayed with broad spectrum pesticides such as organophosphates, carbamates and pyrethroids that can kill natural enemy species as well as pests. Usually natural enemy populations do not appear in significant numbers until aphids begin to be numerous. Among the most important natural enemies are various species of parasitic wasps that lay their eggs inside aphids. The skin of the parasitized aphid turns crusty and golden brown, a form called mummy. The generation time if most parasites are quite short when the weather is warm, so once you begin to see mummies on your plants, the aphid's population is likely to be reduced substantially within a week or two. Many predators also feed on aphids. The most well known are lady beetle, lacewing flies. Naturally occurring predators work best, especially in a small backyard situation. Commercially available lady beetles may give some temporary control when properly handles although most of them will disperse away from your yard within a few days.

Unlike the standard insect method, most aphids are produced from unfertilized eggs—a process called parthenogenesis, and are born alive after a period of development inside the mother's body. The easiest way to introduce the different modes of reproduction is to follow the aphid life history through the year. Although the following scenario is typical of aphids, Aphids have many generations a year. Most aphids in reproduce asexually through out most or all of the year with adult females giving birth to live offspring (often as many as 12 per day) without mating.

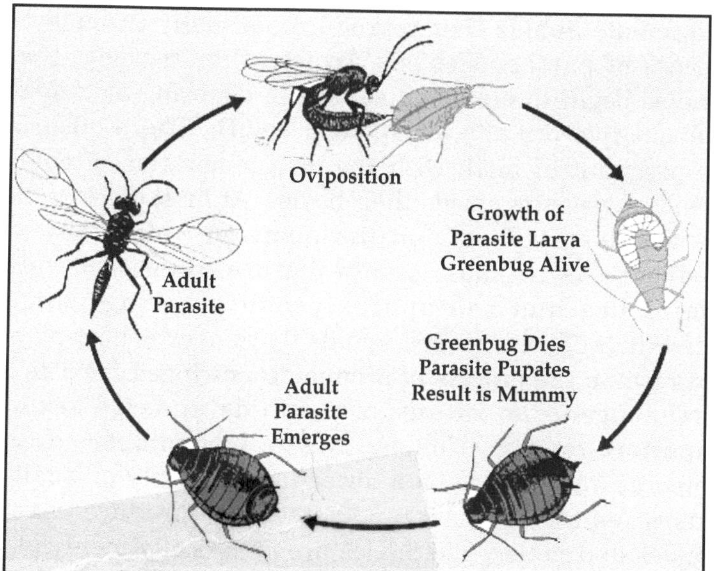

The Life Cycle of an Aphid Parasite, Lysiphlebus Testaceipes

Life Cycle of Common Aphids

Young aphids are called nymphs. They molt, shedding their skins about four times before becoming adults. There is no pupal stage to survive harsh weather. In some case, these eggs are laid on an alternative host, usually a perennial plant, for winter survival. When the weather is warm many species of aphids can develop from newborn nymph to reproducing adult in 7 to 8 days. Because each adult can produce up to 100 offspring in a matter of a week, aphid populations can increase with great speed. Aphid reproduction alternates between a sexual phase and an asexual phase. Most aphids are females produced asexually with males (also produced asexually) appearing in the fall to produce winter eggs. When aphids mate, fertilized eggs are produced and the offspring follow the same genetic mixing that other animals do.

Some aphids use different reproductive cycles in the spring what we explained in above, fertilized eggs hatch into female aphids that reproduce asexually through the process of parthenogenesis. In less than a week, these females begin to produce live female offspring at the rate of about five per day for about a month. These offspring are pregnant at birth with the next generation of aphids already developing inside their bodies. At first, these aphids are wingless and stay on the plant on which they are produced. As the host plants mature, their food value diminishes and the aphids produce spring winged individuals. These winged aphids fly to nearby host plants and resume the process of producing unwinged females by parthenogenesis. In autumn, aphids undergo sexual, oviparous reproduction. A change in photoperiod and temperature, or perhaps a lower food quantity or quality, causes females to parthenogenetically produce sexual females and males. The males are genetically identical to their mothers except that they have one less sex chromosome. These sexual aphids may lack wings or even mouthparts. Sexual females and males mate, and females lay eggs that develop outside the mother. The eggs endure the winter and emerge as winged or wingless females the following spring. This is, for example, the life cycle of the rose aphid (*Macrosiphum rosae*, or less commonly *Aphis rosae*), which may be considered typical of the family. However in warm environments, such as in the tropics or in a greenhouse, aphids may go on reproducing asexually for many years. Some species produce winged females in the summer, sometimes in response to low food quality or quantity. The winged females migrate to start new colonies on a new plant, often of quite a different kind. For example, the apple aphid (*Aphis Mali*), after producing many generations of wingless females on its typical food-plant, gives rise to winged forms which fly away and settle on grass or corn-stalks. Some aphids have telescoping generations. That is, the parthenogenetic, viviparous female has a daughter within her, who is already parthenogenetically producing her own daughter. Thus a female's diet can affect the body size and birth rate of more than two generations

Mutualism with Ants

Some species of ants "farm" aphids, protecting them on the plants they eat, eating the honeydew that the aphids release from the terminations of their alimentary canals. This is a "mutualistic relationship". These "dairying ants" "milk" the aphids by stroking them with their antennae. Therefore, sometimes aphids are called "ant cows. Some farming ant species gather and store the aphid eggs in their nests over the winter. In the spring, the ants carry the newly hatched aphids back to the plants. Some species of dairying ants (such as the European yellow meadow ant, *Lasius flavus*) manage large "herds" of aphids that feed on roots of plants in the ant colony. Queens that are leaving to start a new colony take an aphid egg to find a new herd of underground aphids in the new colony. These farming ants protect the aphids by fighting off aphid predators. An interesting variation in ant-aphid relationships involves Lycaenid butterflies and the Myrmica ants. For example, *Niphanda fusca* butterflies lay eggs on plants where ants tend herds of aphids. The eggs hatch as caterpillars which feed on the aphids. The ants do not defend the aphids from the caterpillars, but carry the caterpillars to their nest. In the nest, the ants feed the caterpillars, which produce honeydew for the ants. When the caterpillars reach full size, they crawl to the colony entrance and form cocoons. After two weeks, butterflies emerge and take flight.

5 Bed Bugs

Bed bugs are blood-sucking in the family Cimicidae. Both nymphs and adults feed on humans mostly at night, a time when it is difficult to detect their stealthy habits. *Cimex lectularius* is a cosmopolitian, or widely distributed, species most frequently found in the northern temperate climates of North America, Europe, and Central Asia. It occurs more sporadically in southern temperate regions. In tropical regions, *C. hemipterus* is the dominant species, but this species does not occur in California. The most common species found in California is *C. lectularius.* The growth and development of *C. lectularius* is optimal when it feeds on humans; however this insect also feeds on their species of mammals and birds found near the home including chickens, mice, rats and rabbits. Untill recently, bed bug infestations were thought to be associated primarily with crowded and dilapidated housing. However, such infestations have undergone resurgence and can be found even in the finest hotel and living accommodations. The reasons for the resurgence are not totally understood but appear to involve increased human travel. Ease of movement of infested luggage and items, and changes in the pesticides available to control this pest.

Identification and Life Cycle

Adult bed bugs are oval, wingless, about 1/5 inch long and rusty red or manogamy. Their bodies are flattened, they have well developed antennae, their compound eyes are small, and the area behind the head (the prothorax) expands forward on either side of the head. The immatures appear identical to the adults except for their smaller size, thinner outer skeleton (cuticle) and lighter, yellowish-white colour. Bed bugs are readily distinguished from another common blood sucking species, conenose bugs by their smaller size, more rounded shape and lack of wings as adults. Consense or kissing bugs may be up to ¾ inch long.

Female bed bugs lay 200 to 500 tiny, white eggs in batches of 10 to 50 on rough surfaces such as wood or paper. Glue-like material covers the eggs, which hatch in about 10 days. After hatching occurs, the eggshells frequently remain stuck in place. There are five progressively larger nymphal stages, each requiring a single blood meal before molting to the next stage. The entire lifecycle from egg to adult requires anywhere from 5 weeks to 4 months, depending on temperature and availability of food (blood). When temperature is the range of 70° to 82° F, development occurs most rapidly. Nymphs and adults generally fed at night and hide in cervices during the day. Common hiding places include seams in mattresses and box springs, cracks in bed frames, under loose wallpaper, behind picture frames and inside furniture and upholstery. Occasionaly people pick up bed bugs in theatres or on buses and trains. They also can bring them into their home on clothing, bedding, luggage, or firewood. Bed bugs can go without feeding for 80 to 140 days. Older stages of nymphs can survive longer without feeding than younger ones, and adults have survived without food for as long as 550 days. A bed bug can take six times its weight in blood and feeding can take 3 to 10 minutes. Adults live about 10 months and there can be up to 3 to 4 generations of bed bugs per year.

Bee and Wasp Stings

Nearly everyone has been stung by an insect at one time or another in their life. It is an unpleasant experience that people hope not to repeat, but for most people the damage inflicted is only temporary pain. Only a very limited portion of the population (one to two people out of 1000) is allergic or hypersensitive to bee or wasp stings. This publication is about stings from bees and wasps, but the information also pertains to stings from fire ants as well. Stinging insects are limited to the order Hymenoptera, which includes wasps, bees and ants. The stinger is a modified egg-laying apparatus, so only females can sting. Most hymenopterans live solitary lives and their behaviour is more likely to be fight than fight. Social hymenopterans, including yellow jackets, honey bees, bumble bees and fire ants, have individual in the colony whose task it is to defend the nest. If the nest is disturbed, these individuals will defend it vigorously. In addition, foraging members of the colony will also sting if they are distributed or injured as they go about their activities. Some, such as the yellow jacket, are much more liable to attack than others. The africanized honey bee is closely related to the European honey bee. However, Africanize honey bees are less predictable and more defensive than European honey bees. They are more likely to defend a greater numbers than European honey bee.

Single Stings

Stingers are effective weapons because they deliver venom that causes pain when injected into the skin. The major chemical responsible for the pain of a honey bee sting called melittin. It stimulates the nerve endings of pain receptors in the skin. The result is a very painful sensation, which begins as a sharp pain that lasts a few minutes and then becomes a dull ache. Even up to a few days later the tissue may still be sensitive to the touch. The body responds to stings by liberating fluid from the blood to flush venom components from the area. This causes redness and swelling at the sting site. If this is not the first time that the person has been stung by that species of insect, it is likely that the immune system will recognize the venom and enhance the disposal procedure. This can lead to very large swelling around the sting site or in a whole portion of the body. The area is quite likely to itch. Oral and topical antihistamines should help prevent or reduce the itching and swelling. Try not to rub or scratch the sting site, because microbes from the surface of the skin could be introduced into the wound and result in an infection. When the sting is caused by a honey bee, the stinger usually remains in the skin when the insect leaves because the stinger is barbed. Remove the stinger as quickly as possible because venom continues to enter the skin from the stinger for 45 to 60 seconds following a sting. Much has been written about the proper way to remove a bee stinger, but new information indicates that it doesn't matter how you get it out as long as it is removed as soon as possible. If removed within 15 seconds of the sting, the severity of the sting is reduced. After the stinger is removed, wash the wound and treat it. Several over-the-counter products or simply a cold compress can be used to alleviate the pain of a sting. Aerosol or cream anti histamine preparations that contain a skin coolant can also help. If the sting is followed by severe symptoms, or if it occurs on the neck or mouth, seek medical attention immediately because swelling in these areas of the body can cause suffocation.

6 Carpenter Bee

Identification

Most carpenter bees, Xylocopa species are large and robust insects resembling bumble bees. They are usually about one inch long and colored a mettalic blue-black with green or purplish reflections. They differ from bumble bees in that their abdomen is shiny with fringes of hairs on some segments. Males of some species are lighter coloured, ranging into golden or buff hues.

Life Cycle

Female carpenter bees bore into sound wood or sometimes into decaying wood to make nests. Nests usually consist of tunnels ½ inch in diameter and 6 to 10 inches deep that are partitioned into several chambers, each containing an egg and a supply of food (pollen). Carpenter bees may use old tunnels for their nests, which they sometimes enlarge; several bees may use a common entry hole connecting to different tunnels. Over a period of time, tunnels may extend as far as 10 feet into wood timbers. Tunnels are vacated after the brood's larval and pupal stages complete their development. Development from egg to adult may take about three months. Carpenter bees over winter as adults, often in old tunnels, and there is only one generation a year.

In several species, the females live alongside their own daughters or sisters, creating a sort of social group. They use wood bits to form partitions between the cells in the nest. A few species bore holes in wood dwellings. Since the tunnels are near the surface, structural damage is generally minor or nonexistent. Carpenter bees can be important pollinators on open-faced flowers, even obligate pollinators on some, such as the Maypop (*Passiflora incarnata*), though many species are also known to "rob" nectar by slitting the sides of flowers with deep corollas. In the United States, there are two eastern species, *Xylocopa virginica,* and *Xylocopa micans*, and three other species that are primarily western in distribution, *Xylocopa varipuncta*, *Xylocopa tabaniformis* orpifex and *Xylocopa californica*. *X. virginica* is by far the more widely distributed species. Some are often mistaken for a bumblebee species, as they can be similar in size and coloration, though most carpenter bees have a shiny abdomen, while in bumblebees the abdomen is completely clothed with dense hair. Males of some species have a white or yellow face, where the females do not; males also often have much larger eyes than the females, which relates to their mating behaviour. Male bees are often seen hovering near nests, and will approach nearby animals. However, males are harmless since they do not have a stinger. Female carpenter bees are capable of stinging, but they are docile and rarely sting unless caught in the hand or otherwise directly provoked. Many Old World carpenter bees have a special pouch-like structure on the inside of their first metasomal tergite called the acarinarium where certain species of mites (*Dinogamasus* spp.) reside as commensals. The exact nature of the relationship is not fully understood, though in other bees that carry mites, the mites are beneficial, feeding either on fungi in the nest, or on other, harmful mites.

Carpenter bees are traditionally considered solitary bees, though some species have simple social nests in which mothers and daughters may cohabit. However, even solitary species tend to be gregarious, and often several will nest near each other. It has been occasionally reported that when females cohabit, there may be a division of labor between them, where one female may spend most of her time as a guard within the nest, motionless and near the entrance, while another female spends most of her time foraging for provisions. Carpenter bees make nests by tunneling into wood, vibrating their bodies as they rasp their mandibles against the wood, each nest having a single entrance which may have many adjacent tunnels. The entrance is often a perfectly circular 16 millimetres (0.63 in) hole on the underside of a beam or tree limb. Carpenter bees do not eat wood. They discard the bits of wood, or re-use particles to build partitions between cells. The tunnel functions as a nursery for brood and storage for the pollen/nectar upon which the brood subsists. The provision masses of some species are among the most complex in shape of any group of bees; whereas most bees fill their brood cells with a soupy mass, and others form simple spheroidal pollen masses, *Xylocopa* form elongate and carefully sculpted masses that have several projections which keep the bulk of the mass from coming into contact with the cell walls, sometimes resembling an irregular caltrop. The eggs are very large relative to the size of the female, and are some of the largest eggs among all insects. There are two very different mating systems that appear to be common in carpenter bees, and often this can be determined simply by examining specimens of the males of any given species. Species in which the males have large eyes are characterized by a mating system where the males either search for females by patrolling, or by hovering and waiting for passing females, whom they then pursue. In the other type of mating system, the males often have very small heads, but there is a large, hypertrophied glandular reservoir in the mesosoma, which releases pheromones into the airstream behind the male while it flies or hovers. The pheromone advertises the presence of the male to females.

7 Oakworm

The oakworm belongs family Dioptidae is one many species of caterpillars that feed on oaks. It is the most important oak-feeding caterpillar throughout its range, which extends along the coast live oak (*Quercus agrifolia*) in the san Fransico Bay and Monterey Bay regions. Populations vary unpredictably year to year from high to undetectably low. Healthy oaks generally tolerate extensive loss of leaves (defoliation) without serious harm, so treatment to control oakworms usually is not recommended.

Identification

The adult called an oak moth is a uniform tan to gray or silver colour and is distinguished by its prominent wing veins. The body is about ½ inches long and the wingspread is about ¼ inches. Unlike females, males have feathery antennae. The female lays tiny, round eggs in group of about two or three dozen, mostly on the underside of leaves. The eggs initially are white built develop red centres that become pinkish to brownish gray before hatching into larval stage (caterpillars) Despite their common name, young oakworms are not wormlike but are small, yellowish green caterpillar with large, brown heads and dark stripes on their sides. Older caterpillars vary in colour, commonly dark with prominent, lengthwise yellow or olive stripes. Caterpillar range from 1/10 inch long when newly hatched to about one inch when fully grown. In pupal stage they are white, yellowish or pinkish moth black markings, ½ inch long and suspend from limbs, leaves, trunks or objects near trees. Inside the colourful pupal case, also called a chrysalis, the oakworm develops into a moth.

Other Leaf-eating Species

The fruit tree leaf roller (*Archips argyrospila*) is the most common defoliator of oaks in the warmer central valley of California. Larvae are green with brown or black heads and ¾ to one inch length at maturity. When distrubuted, they often wiggle vigorously and drop from leaves while suspended on silken threads. Larvae feed on buds and developing leaves, webbing them together to form a protective case. Initial damage includes leaf skeletonization. As the larvae mature, they may consume entire leaves. Tussock moths (*Orgyia specise*) and tent caterpillars (*Malacosoma species*) also feed on oaks throught the state. Unlike the greenish, relatively smooth surface of California oakworm and fruit tree leafroller larvae, tent caterpillar and tussock moth larvae are quite hairy.

Life Cycle

Two oak worm generations a year occur in Northern California as described below. A third generation sometimes occur at warmer and inland sites and in Northern California in years if uncommonly warm, dry winters. Insect development in southern California and other warmer sites especially variable and oak moths may appear almost any time from March through November.

Biological Control

Predaotors, parasites and natural outbreaks of disease sometimes kill enough oak worms to control populations *Predators*. Predators include birds, spiders and predatory insects. Green lacewing larvae (chrysopa and Chrysoperla species), pirate bugs (*Orius species*), the spined soldier bug

(*Podisus maculiventris*), snd yellow jackets (Vespula and Dolichovespula species) are important oak worm predators. Green lacewing larvae, adults and nymphs of pirate bugs and soldier bugs feed on oakworm eggs, larvae and pupae ikpaling prey with their tubular sucking mouth parts. Yellow jackets carry oakworms back to their nests, where the wasp larvae eat them.

Parasitic Wasps

Two small wasps (*Itoplectis behrensii*, family Ichneumonidae and *Brachymeria ovata*, family Chacididae) are reported to be the most important parasites. In both species, the wasps immature stages - egg, larva and pupa- occur within oak worm pupae. An irregularly rounded hole chewed by an emerging adult wasp can be seen in parasite-killed oakworm pupae. The adult *Brachymeria ovata* is stout, black and yellow and about ¼ inch long with a enlarged rear basal leg segments. The *Itoplectis behrensii* adult is slender with long narrow abdomen and a body length of about ¼ to 2/3 inch. This wasp is mostly black but has long legs that are orange with yellow and black bands.

Parasitic Flies

At least two parasitic Tachinid flies (*Actia flavipes* and *Hyphantrophaga virillis* family Tachinadae) kill oakworm larvae. The female fly lays one or more eggs on an oakworm. The emerging larvae bore down and feed inside the oakworm. As the parasitized caterpillar begins to pupate, the fly larvae inside kill their host and emerge to form oblong, reddish to dark brown pup[al cases that may be seen on or beneath oaks. The dry, deflated skins of Tachinid-killed oakworms often remain attached to twigs or bark.

Pathogens

Naturally occuring pathogens including a nuclear polyhedrosis virus (NPV) and a fungus (*Beauveria bassiana*) often kill oakworms. Symptoms of virus infection are dark, soft, limp larval carcasses hanging from foliage or twigs; carcases eventually.

8 Olive Fruit Fly

The olive fruit fly, *Bactrocera oleae* this belongs to Diptera, Tephritidae first was recorded in California in October 1998 when a single female fly was captured in west Los Angeles. By fell 1999, olive fruit flies had been captured in seven additional countries including Tulare country, in the San Joaquin valley, the leading producer of table olives growing areas of California and threatens virtually all commercial and fruit-bearing ornamental olive plantings.

Impact

The olive fruit poses a severe economic threat for the state's commercial olive growers. The larvae (maggots) of the olive fruit fly feed inside the fruit, destroying the pulp and allowing the entry of secondary bacteria and fungi that rot the fruit and degrade the quality of the oil. Feeding damage can cause premature fruit drop and reduce fruit quality fro both table olive and olive oil production. Large numbers of rooting fruit on the ground can create an unwelcome mess, especially in landscaped situations. In areas of the world where the olive fruit fly is well established, it has been responsible fro crop losses of 100 per cent of some table cultivars and upto 80 per cent of oil value. It is considered the most devasting insect pest of olives in the mediterean region, where it has occurred for more than 2000 years. For table olive growers, the presence of even a few infested fruit can lead to rejection of an entire crop. Some infestation can be tolerated in olive fruit can lead to rejection if an entire crop. Some infestation can be tolerated in olive fruit used for oil production as long as the fruit are not rotten. Harvesting early and pressing fruit quickly a faster harvest will reduce off-flavour changes caused by olive fruit fly injury. Ornamental olive trees can serve as a source of olive fruit flies infesting commercial plantings, especially as adult flies are capable of flying long distances.

Identification

The adult olive fruit fly is about ¼ inch long. The head, thorax, and abdomen are brown with darker markings and several white or yellow patches on the top sides of the thorax. Its wings are positioned horizontally and are held away from the body. Olive fruit flies may be distinguished from related fruit flies by the presence of black spots on the wing tips and the lack of banding across the wings that occurs the wings that occurs in most related species such as walnut husk fly, apple maggot and medditerean fruit fly may be distinguished from males by the presence of an ovipositor, a dark coloured pointed structure at the end of the abdomen, which is used to pierce olive fruit and lay eggs. Usually only egg is laid per fruit. However, multiple eggs may be laied in olive varieties that produce large fruit; females prefer large-fruited varieties to smaller-fruited ones fro egg laying. Larvae are yellowish white, legless maggots with pointed heads. When first hatched they are immediately below the surface, tiny and difficult to see. After they have been feeding for a while they are easier to locate, especially when the fruit has begun to rot.

Life Cycle

The life cycle of the olive fruit fly is closely linked to the seasonal development of its main host, the cultivated olive (olea europea) and to the local climate. In mild coastal areas of California, adult flies remain active year round and the eggs and maggots can be found through out the year in fruit left on the ground or on trees. In land areas of California, adult flies emerge from March to May and attack olives remaining on trees from the previous season. During early summer (June) as temperatures and few mature fruit remain on trees, female flies do not lay eggs. Although few olives are present from the previous crop to host the egg laying, the adults remain active and they may disperse to new locations such as citrus orchids or vine yards. By late June to the beginning of July as the new olive crop develops, females begin to lay eggs and are attracted to the fruit. Although eggs may be laid in small fruit, the larvae do not successfully develop until the ripening fruit grows to sufficient size. Eggs are laid just under the fruit's skin. Often creating a dimple or brown spot. Under laboratory conditions, an individual female olive fruit fly may lay 10 to 40 eggs per day and from 200 to 500 eggs in her life time. Larvae that develop during early to midsummer pupate in the fruit and emerge later in the season as adults. Larvae produced during fall leave the fruit and pupate in the soil where they spend the winter; however, some maggots overwinter in fruit left on trees and pupate in spring. Multiple generations occur through out summer and fall. In summer the flies can complete a generation in as little as 30 to 35 days, given optimum temperatures (68° to 86°F).

The olive fruit fly has no true period of dormancy, and all stages of the insect can occur during winter. The lower and upper activity thresholds for the adult olive fruit fly are about 60° F and 95°F respectively. Below and above these thresholds they are not very active. Eggs hatch in 2 to 3 days, and larvae develop in about 20 days during summer and fall. Pupal development requires 8 to 10 days during summer but may take as long as 6 months in winter. Hot (95° to 105°F), dry conditions reduce the buildup of olive fruit fly populations. Fruit fly eggs and first instar maggots can experience relatively high mortality during hot, dry weather. Adult flies also may die during periods of high temperature if adequate water and food are not available. High olive fruit fly populations have been observed in both coastal and inland areas.

9 White Flies

White flies are tiny, sap sucking insects that are frequently abundant in vegetable and ornamental plantings. They excrete sticky honeydew and cause yellowing or death of leaves. Outbreaks often occur when the natural biological control is disrupted. Management is difficult.

Identification and Life cycle

Whiteflies usually occur in groups on the undersides of leaves. They derive their name from the mealy, white wax covering the adult's wings and body. Adults are tiny insects with yellowish bodies and whitish wings. Although adults of some species have distinctive wing markings, many species are most readily distinguished in the last nymphal (immature) stage, which is wingless Table 9.1 shows the following the host plants and name of the pest that is white flies.

White flies develop rapidly in warm weather, and populations can build up quickly in situations where natural enemies are destroyed and weather is favourable. Most whiteflies, especially the most common pest species - greenhouse whitefly (*Trialeurodes vaporariorum*) and silverleaf or sweetpotato whiteflies (bemisia species) – have a wide host range that includes many weeds and crops.

Table 9.1: Major Economic Hosts of Some Common Whiteflies

Whitefly	Host plants and characteristics
Ash whitefly (*Siphoninus phillyreae*)	**Host plants**.: Many broad leaved trees and shruns including ash, citrus, bradford pear and other flowering fruit trees, pomegranate, redbud. **Characterstics**: Fourth-instar nymphs have a very thick band of wax down the back and fringe of tiny tubes, each with aliquid droplet at the ens. Adults are white.
Bandedwinged whitefly (*Trialeurodes abutilonea*)	**Host plants**: very broad including cotton, cucubits, other vegetables **Characterstics**: Fourth-instar nymphs have short, waxy filaments around their edges. Adult have brownish bands across the wings and their body is gray.
Citrus whitefly (*Dialeuruodes citri*)	**Host plants**: citrus, gardenia, ash, ficus, pomegranate **Characterstics**: Fourth-instar nymphs have no fringe around their edges but have a distinctive Y-shape on their backs. Adults are white.
Crown whitefly (*Aleuroplatus coronata*)	**Host plants**: oak, chestnut **Characterstics**: Fourth-instar nymphs are black with large amounts of white wax arranged in a crown like pattern. Adults are white.
Giant whitefly (*Aleurodicus dugesii*)	**Host plants:** begonia, hibiscus, giant bird of paradise, orchid tree, banana, mulberry, vegetables and many ornamentals; currently only in Southern California **Charctersics**: adults are up to 0.19-inch long. They leavespirals of wax on leaves. Nymphs have long filaments of wax that can be up to 2 inches long and give leaves a bearded appearance. For more information see pest notes: giant White fly listed in references.

(Contd...)

Greenhouse whitefly (*Trialeurodes vaporariorum*)	**Host plants**: very broad including most vegetables and herbaceous ornamentals **Characterstics**: fourth-instar nymphs have very long waxy filaments and a marginal fringe. Adults have whit wing and a yellow surface or substrate
Iris whitefly (*Aleyrodes spiraeoides*)	**Host plants**: iris, gladious, many vegetables, cotton and other herbaceous plants **Charctersics**: fourth-instar nymphs have no fringe or waxy filaments but true located near distinctive circles of wax where egg laying took place. Adults have a dot on each wing and are quite waxy.
Mulberry whitefly (*Tetraleurodes mori*)	**Host plants**: citrus, other trees **Characterstics**: nymphs have blackish, oval bodies with white, waxy fringe.
Silverleaf and sweet potato white flies (*Bemisia argentifolii* and *B. tabaci*)	**Host plants**: very broad including many herbaceous whiteflies some woody plants such as cotton, cucurbits, tomatoes, peppers, lanatana, cole crops and hibiscus **Characterstics**: Fourth-instar nymphs have no waxy filaments or marginal fringe. Adults have white wings and yellow body; they hold their wings slightly tilted to surface or substrate.
Wooly whitefly (*Aleurothrixus flooccosus*)	**Host plants**: citrus, eugina **Characterstics**: Nymphs are covered with fluffy, waxy filaments

In many parts of California, they breed all year, moving from one host to another asplants are harvested or dry up. Whiteflies normally lay their tiny, oblong eggs on the under of leaves. The eggs hatch, and the young whiteflies gradually increase in size through four nymphal stages called instars. The first nymphal stage (crawler) is barley visible even with a hand lens. The crawlers move around for several hours, then settle and remain immobile. Later nymphal stages are oval and flatened like small scale insects. The legs and antennae are greatly reduced and older nymphs do not move. The winged adult emerges from the last nymphal stage (for conveinence sometimes incorrectly called a pupa). All stages feed by sucking plant juices from leaves and excreting excess liquid as drops of honeydew as they feed.

Damage

Whiteflies suck phloem sap. Large populations can cause leaves to turn yellow, appear dry, or fall off plants. Like aphids, whiteflies excrete honeydew, so leaves may be sticky or covered with black sooty mold. The honeydew attracts ants, which interfere with the activities of natural enemies that may control whiteflies and other pests. Feeding by the immature silver leaf whitefly, *Bemisia argentifolii*, can cause serious losses in some vegetable crops. Some whiteflies transmit viruses to certain vegetable crops. With the notable exception of the citrus whitefly, whiteflies are not normally a problem in fruit trees, but several whiteflies can be problems on ornamental trees (see Table 9.1). Low levels of whiteflies are not usually damaging. Adults by themselves will not cause significant damage unless they are transmitting a plant pathogen. Generally, plant losses do not occur unless there is a significant population of whitefly nymphs.

Management

Management of heavy whitefly infestations is very difficult. Whiteflies are not well controlled with any available insecticides. The best strategy is to prevent problems from developing in your garden to the extent possible. In many situations, natural enemies will provide adequate control of whiteflies; outbreaks may occur if natural enemies that provide biological control of whiteflies are disrupted by insecticide applications, dusty conditions or interference by ants. Avoid or remove plants that repeatedly host high populations of whiteflies. In gardens white fly population in the early stages of population development can be held down by against programme of removing infested leaves, vaccuming adults, or hosing down (syringing) with water sprays. Alumimum foil or reflective mulches can repel whiteflies from vegetable gardens and sticky traps can be used to monitor or at high levels, reduce whitefly numbers. If you choose to use insecticides, insecticidal soaps or oils such as neem oil may reduce but not eliminate populations.

Biological Control

Whiteflies have many natural enemies and outbreaks frequently occur when these natural enemies have been distributed or destroyed by pesticides, dust build up or other factors. General predators include lacewings, big eyed bugs and minute pirate bugs. Several small lady beetles including *Clitostethus arcuatus* (on ash white fly)and scale predators such as Scymnus or Chilocorus species, and the Asian multicoloured lady beetle, *Harmonia axyridis*, feed on white flies. Whiteflies have a number of naturally occurring parasites that can be very important in controlling some species. *Encarsia* sp. Parasites are commercially available for release in greenhouse situations; however they are not well adapted for survival in temperate zones. An exception is the use of parasite releases for bayberry white fly in citrus in America. You can evaluate the degree of natural parasitization in your plants by checking empty whitefly pupal xcases. Those that were parasitized will have a T-shaped exit hole. Whitefly nymphs can sometimes be checked for parasitization before emergence by noting a darkening in their colour. However, some whitefly parasites do not turn hosts black and many whitefly nymphs that occur on ornamentals are black in their unparasitized state.

Avoiding the use of insecticides that kill natural enemies is a very imporatnt aspect of whitefly management. Products containing carbyl, pyrethroids, diazinon or foliar sprays of imidacloprid can be particularly disruptive. Control of duct and ants,which protect whiteflies from their natural enemies, can also be important especially in citrus or other trees.

10 Clearwing Moths

The larvae of several species of clearwing moths in the insect family sesiidae are important wood boring pests in landscapes. Hosts include alder, ash, birch fir, oak, pine, poplar, sycamore, willow and stone fruit trees such as apricot, cherry, peach and plum. Larvae that closely resemble those of clearwing moths include the American plum borer, a serious boring pest of hosts that include fruit and nut trees, mountain ash, olive and syncamore. Other common wood boring pests in landscapes include bark beetles (family: Scoltidae), longhorned (Cerambycidae) and roundheaded borers (buprestidae).

Identification

Dying limbs rough gnarled bark and sawdust like frass (insect excrement) are good indications that trees are infested with wood boring insects. When clearwing moth larvae bore beneath tree bark, they push frass from their tunnels; the frass is sometimes mixed with gummy tree exdate. Small piles or ascattedred dusting of frass is sometimes mixed with gummy tree exudate. Small piles or ascattered dustings of frass mark the location of tunnel openings. The larvae are 1 to 1-½ inches long at maturity and have a dark brown head and a whitish to pink body that darkens before pupating. After larvae mature and pupa and moths emerge, empty brownish pupal cases may be observed protruding from bark or on the ground near the base of the tree. Clearwing moth adults have long, narrow front wings and shorter, wider hind wings. The hind wings and in some species the front wings are mostly clear. These moths fly during the day or at twilight, and their yellow and black colouring resembles that of paper wasps or yellow jackets. Adult display wasp like behaviour by intermittently running while rapidly fluttering their wings. The differ in colour depending on species and sex. They are often yellow, orange, or red on black or dark blue.

Life Cycle

Clearwing moths develop through four stages: egg, larva, pupa, and adult. Adults do not directly damage plants and live only about one week. Soon after emerging from the pupal case, female moths emit a pheromone that attracts males. After mating, the female deposits her tiny reddish to pale pink eggs in cracks, cervices and rough or wounded areas on bark. Eggs hatch in about 1 to 4 weeks. The newly emerged larvae bore into the bark, camnium, or heartwood of the host tree. Mature larvae pupate beneath bark, except for the peach tree borer, which pupates in soil. The species discussed here have one generation per year except for the western poplar clearwing, which requires 1 to 2 years to complete one generation. At least six species of clearwing moths are frequent pests of broad leaf trees and shrubs in and are covered in this publication. Other common species include the sequoia pitch moth (*Synanthedon sequoiae*) and Douglas-fir pitch moth (*Synanthedon novaroensis*), which attack pine, sprice.

American Hornet Moth

The American hornet moth, sesia tibialis, closely resembles the western poplar clearwing disccused below, and its infested many of the same plants. Host include aspen, cottonwood, popular and willow. It ranges from New England to the Pacific Coast states. American hornet moth is mostly blackish blue with some brown, orange or yellow. Larvae of the ash borer, Poosesia syringae, also known as the lilac or lilac-ash borer, mine the wood of ash, lilac, olive and privet. This clearwing moth occurs through out the United States, but varies in appearance and behaviour depending on location. In west, the male ash borer has long brownish legs and black body with narrow yellow bands. In United States, ash borer occurs primarily in central valley, where it attacks the tree trunks and limbs, mostly within about 5 or 10 feet of the ground. Infestations occur most often at sites on the tree where bark has been injured by pruning, improper staking or previous generations of ash borer.

11 Spiders

Many people fear or dislike spiders but, for the most part, spiders are beneficial because of their role as predators of insects and other arthropods and most cannot harm people. Spiders that might injure people for example, black widows generally spend most of their time hidden under furniture or boxes, or in woodpiles, corners or crevices. The spiders commonly seen out in the open during the day are unlikely to bite people.

Identification

Spiders resemble insects and sometimes are confused with them, but they are arachnids, not insects. Spiders have eight legs and two body parts a head region (ccphalothorax) and an abdomen. They lack wings and antennae. Although spiders often arc found on plants, they eat mainly insects, other spiders and related arthropods, not plants. Most spiders have toxic venom, which they use to kill their prey. However, only these spiders whose venom typically causes a serious reaction in humans are called "poisonous" spiders, see the sidebar: spider bites.

Some Spider Families in India Agelenadae, Funnel Weavers or Grass Spiders

This is type of the Spider which sit-and-wait predators feed during the day and night on the ground in most types of vegetation, including low-growing plants and trees. Spin funnel-shaped webs, often with several-inch-wide, flat extention covering plants or soil. The spider waits in the hole of its web. When it detects vibration from an insect that flew or walked into the web. When it detects vibrations from an insect that flew or walked into web, the spider runs out, captures and bites the prey, then carries it back into the funnel to be eaten. Webs on low vegetation become conspicuous in morning light after collecting dew. Funnel weavers have six or eight eyes, all about the same size, arranged in two rows.This family consists of 300 species.

Araneidae, Orb Weavers or Garden Spiders

Feed on insects that fly, fall or are blown into web. Elaborate silken webs are spun in concentric circles. Spiderlings often make symmetrical webs; mature spiders may spin a more specialized design that is helpful in identifying certain species. the spider rests at the center of its web or hides in a shelter near the edge, waiting for prevent to become entangled. Orb weavers generally have poor vision and rely on web vibrations to locate and identify prey. There are about 200 species coming under this family.

Clubionidae (including Corinnidae), Sac Spiders or Two Clawed Hunting Spiders

Stalk and capture prey that is walking or resting on surfaces. They spin silken tubes or sacs under bark, among leaves, and in low plants or on the ground, where they hide during the day or retreat after hunting. Commonly they are nocturnal, medium-sized, pale spiders with few markings. There are around 200 species found all over the world.

Linyphiidae (Microphantidae) Dwarf Spiders

Prey on insects that fall, walk or land in their web. Diurnal (day active) spiders occurring in the plant canopy and among litter on the ground. They produce sheet like web on the surface of plants or soil and are common in some field and vegetable crops. Most relatively small several hundred species found on this earth.

Lycosidae, Wolf Spiders

Prey on insects that are walking or resting on the ground, actively hunt in the open during day and night, often observed on the ground in litter and on low vegetation. They occur in burrows and under debris on soil. Instead of spinning webs to catch prey, make a small, thick web where they rest. Have a distinctive pattern of eyes: four small eyes in front in straight row, one middle pair of larger eyes, and one rear pair of widely spaced eyes on top of the head. They are found in 200 species they have long hairy legs. They are usually black and white or string contrasting light and dark, which can make them difficult they are moving.

Oxyopidae, Lynx Spiders

Stalk and capture resting or walking insects. These are active hunters with good vision. Most have spiny legs and a brightly coloured body that tapers sharply toward the rear. They have four pairs of eyes grouped in a hexagon. They are found about 12 species in nature.

Salticidae, Jumping Spiders

These are day active hunters in plants or on the ground. They make no web; instead they stalk and pounce on prey by jumping distances many times their body length. Jumping spiders have a distinctive pattern of eyes in three rows: the first row of four eyes, with large and instinctive middle eyes; a bevond row of two very small to minute eye; and a third row of two medium sized eyes. They usually have an irridescent, mettalic-coloured abdomen and black carapace. About 300 species in North America.

Theridiidae, Combweb, Combweb Weaver, or Comb Footed Spiders

Feed on insects that walk or fly into their webs. Almost always found hanging upside down by their claws in irregularly spun, sticky webs, waiting for prey. The spider is usually concealed in a corner of the web, in a silken tent, or behind debris. This group includes the black widow spider, which produces relatively thick silk that feels rough and sticky. They generally have a sift, round, bulbous abdomen and slender legs without spines. This includes 200 species at present.

Thomisidae, Crab Spiders or Flower Spiders

This is type of the Spider Stalk and capture insects walking or resting on surfaces. These are Diurnal hunters that do not spin webs. Front two pairs of legs are enlarged and extend beyond the side of their flattened body, making them look like tiny crabs. Their small eyes occur in two slightly curved rows, with the top row often much wider than the lower row. This includes around 200 species.

Fleas

Cat fleas (*Ctenocephalides felis*) are fequently encountered in homes and are common pests on domestic cats and dogs. Dog leas (*Ctenocephalides canis*) look like cat fleas. Sticktight fleas (*Echidnophaga gallinacea*) can become a proble when pets frequent areas near poultry. Female sticktight fleas firmly attach themselves around the ears and eyes of their host. Fleas on either cats or dogs in India are most likely cat fleas.

Identification

Adult pleas are very small insects (up to 1/8 inch), so it is difficult tosee a number of the characteristics used to describe them. These reddish brown to black, wingless insects are compressed from side to side so that they look like they are walking “on edge”. They have peircung-sucking mouthparts through which they obtain blood meals from their hosts. Flea larvae are tiny (up to 3/16 inch long), hairy, and wormlike with a distinct, brownish head, but no eyes or legs.

Life Cycle

Female cat fleas remain on the host (unlike most other fleas) and lay about 20 to 30 eggs pre day on the animal. Cat flea eggs are pearly white, oval and about 1/32 inch long. The eggs are smooth; they readily fall from the pet and land on surfaces like bedding and carpenting in the animal's environment. They hatch in about two days. The whitish, wormlike larvae feed on dried blood and excrement produced by adult fleas feeding on the pet. Larval development is normally restricted to protected places where there is at least 75 per cent relative humidity. They feed and crawl around for 5 to 15 days at 70° to 90° F before they build small silken cocoons in which they develop into adult fles (pupate). The pupae are usually covered with local debris for visual camouflage. Flea larvae develop more quickly at high temperatures. At cool temperatures, fully formed fleas may remain in their cocoons for up to 12 months. Warm temperatures and mechanical pressure, caused by walking on the carpet, vaccuming and so on, stimulate emergence from the cocoon. At room temperatures, the entire life cycle may be completed in about 18 days. An adult cat flea generally lives about 30 to 40 days on the host; it is the only stage that feeds on blood. Fleas may be found on pets throughout the year, but numbers tend to increase dramatically during spring and early summer.

Problems Associated with Fleas

The cat fleasis suspected of transmitting murine typhus to humans, but its primary importance is in its annoyance to people and pets. Cat fleas readily try to feed on almost any warm-blodded animal. Some people are bothered by the sesation of fleas walking on their skin, but bites are the major nuisance. Bites tend to be concentrated on the lower legs but can also occur other parts pf the body. The bite consists of a small, central red spot surrounded by ared halo, usually without excessive swelling. Flea bites usually cause minor itching but may become increasingly irritating to people with sensative or reactive skin. Some people and pets suffer from fiea bite allergic dermatitis, characterized by intense itching, hair loss, reddening of the skin and secondary infection. Just one bite may initiate an allergic reaction, and itching may persist up to 5 days after the bite. Cat fleas may also serve as intermediary hosts of dog tapeworms. Cats or dogs may acquire this intestinal parasite while grooming themselves by ingesting adult fleas that contain a cyst of the tapeworm.

Management

The best approach to managing fleas is prevention. New, safer and more effective products aimed at controlling fleas on the pet have node flea managent without pesticide sprays feasible in many situations. Management of fleas on the pet must be accompanied by regular, through cleaning of pet resting areas indoors and outside. Once fleas infest a hom, control will require a vigilant progarm that includes cleaning and traeting infested areas indoors, eliminating fleas on pets and cleaning up and possibly treating shaded outdoor locations where pets rest.

12 Mosquitoes

Mosquito (from the Spanish or Portuguese meaning *little fly*) is a common insect in the family Culicidae (from the Latin *culex* meaning *midge* or *gnat*). Mosquitoes resemble crane flies (family: Tipulidae) and chironomid flies (family Chironomidae), with which they are sometimes confused by the casual observer.

Typical Mosquitoes

Mosquitoes are the most primitive diptera being closely related to midges, gnats and craneflies. Three quarters of all mosquito species live in the hunid tropics and subtorpics where the warm moist climate has favoured the existence of diversity of habitats permitting the evolution of many species. The family Culicidae is separated in to two medically important subfamilies, the Anophelinae and Culicinae. The former being the smaller group includes the vectors of human malaria (Genus: Anopheles) and the later consists of vectors of filarial and viral diseases such as JE, dengue haemorrhagic fever (DHF), yellow fever, filariasis etc. (Genera: Aedes, Culex and Mansonia). In terms of public health importance, about 300 species of mosquitoes in the world play important roles due to their vactorial capacity.

Mosquitoes have been the focus of investigations since the time the first human disease was linked to them. Compared to other insects, they cause more human suffering, serving a cyclic or mechanical but exclusive vectors of five important diseases of man namely dengue, yellow fever, malaria, filariasis, and encephalitis. Among the mosquito genera, Anopheles, Aedes and Culex are very important as they include the principal vectors of malaria, dengue, yellow fever and most of the encephalitis causing arboviruses. More than fourteen mosquito genera are known to harbour arboviruses (arthropod borne viruses). These diseases are major public health concerned in the world.

Among different mosquito vectored diseases, dengue attracted the attention of the health care workers with the emergence of more critical forms, dengue haemorrhagic fever (DHF) and dengue shock syndrome (DSS), which are the most important re-emergent arboviral diseases of the human beings. It is the second most important mosquito borne disease in the world next to malaria. Due to the severe pain caused in the joints and muscles, it is commonly called the 'brake-bone' disease. Four serotypes namely DEN1, DEN2, DEN3 and DEN4 are dengue viruses belonging to the family Flaviviridae. Infection with one serotype confers life long immunity to that particular virus. There is very strong evidence that, the risk of DHF is substantially greater among persons suffering a second dengue infection with a different serotypes. These unique characteristics of dengue viruses make vaccine development, disease surveillance and laboratory diagnosis exceptionally challenging. Dengue has been known clinically since many years and the fatality rate in case of this disease is nil whereas in DHF, it may exceed 13 per cent in some areas.

The global dengue pandemic has intensified during the past two decades and now affects all continents except Antartica. It has become a major international and debilitating health problem affecting the tropical and sub-tropical regions of the world, especially the urban and periurban areas. The conditions responsible for dengue epidemics continue to mount and the global population at risk is estimated to range from 2.5 to 3 billion. World Health Organisation (WHO) currently estimates approximately 50 to 100 million cases of DHF every year spread to over 100 countries of America, Africa, Eastern Meditterranean, South-east Asia and the Western Pacific, the latter two being seriously affected. Formerly thought to be strictly urban, dengue is now recognized as being of significance in rural areas as well in South-east Asia. Since the end of II world war, 38 out of 46 countries of the Asian continent and islands of pacific have experienced dengue and DHF epidemics. All the four serotypes are virtually present in every country of the region. Recent DHF epidemics have occurred in India, Srilanka, Pakistan, Myanmar, China, Thailand, Indonesia, Philippines, Maldives, Cambodia, Laos, Vietnam, Malaysia, Singapore and many islands of the Pacific. DHF is the leading cause of hospitalization and death in children of many countries in Asia and the pacific nations. In the year 2003, 70,959 cases of dengue were reported from Asia, out of which maximum number of cases were from Thailand (24,004), followed by Indonesia (18,797) India with 4720 cases stood fifth in the list.

In India, dengue has been known for over a century. Seasonal and cyclic epidemic pattern of dengue is a recent phenomenon observed in India and Srilanka, identical to the problem detected in Philippines, Thailand and Indonesia. This new dengue paradigm has now screened a firm foothold and has emerged as a major health problem in many parts of the country. Endemicity of DF, DHF and DSS has been recognized for the past several years as the leading cause of death in children. The number of dengue cases ranges from 7 to 16 thousand per annum in India. A maximum of 21,79,996 cases were recorded in 1986. Dengue outbreaks occur annually in India, with most cases are reported from Western and Southern states and the risk of dengue is round the year. In northern states it is primarily occur from April through November. DHF was first recorded in the metropolitan city of Culcutta during 1963. Subsequent outbreaks of dengue fever occurred in cities on the east coast as well as the central, northern and southern parts of the country including an epidemic in Madras during 1989 and 1990. A fairly recent and severe epidemic of DHF/DSS occurred in Delhi and adjoining areas fron August through November 1996. A total of 8900 cases were reported with a death rate of 4.2 per cent. In addition, New Delhi situated in Northern part of India, esperienced outbreaks of different magnitude due to different viral serotypes in 1967, 1970, 1982, 1996 and 2003. All these outbreaks occurred during the monsoons (August-November) and subsided with onset of winter, However, an episode of dengue fever occur in Jalore town, southwest of Rajasthan State in April and May 1985. This was the first reported outbreak of dengue in the arid zone of west Rajasthan during dry season in contrast to there parts of India where the outbreak follow heavy rains.

After the 1996 episode, there was a decline in the incidence of dengue. With outbreaks in the state of Rajasthan (1452 cases and 35 deaths), Tamilnadu (816 cases and 8 deaths), Haryana (260 cases and 5 deaths) and Karnataka (220 cases and no death) during 2001, there was an increase in the number of cases and deaths (41%) was noticed during 2002, as compared to 2001. However, during 2003, cases and deaths increased to the tune of 62.7 per cent and 60 per cent respectively have been recorded. Since 1997, this was the highest number of cases and death in the country. The disease has been spread at an alarming magnitude in the southern state as well with Kerala state registering 3155 cases and 63 deaths. Karnataka state where the present study spot is situated stands second in the list with 1201 cases and 6 deaths during 2003. The total number of cases and deaths recorded in India during 2003 was 4720 and 78 respectively. According to WHO (SEARO) in India number of Dengue cases were above 12000 in 2005 with CFR (Case Fatality Rate) nearly 1.4 per cent.

All the four serotypes of dengue virus are transmitted through the bites of the infective female mosquito of the genus, Aedes, which has been known since 1903. By 1926, investigations had incriminated Ae. albopictus was also as dengue vector. Since then, over 20 species of mosquitoes, all belonging to the genus *Aedes* have either been proved or suspected as the vector of dengue virus, by isolating the virus in nature and/or by experimental studies. *Ae. albopictus* has been found to be the most important vector in epidemics worldwide and is the principal vector of DF and DHF in southeast Asia (WHO, 1999). *Ae. albopictus* is the secondary vector, important in the maintainance of dengue viruses in Asia and Americas. *Ae. scutellaris, Ae. africanus, Ae. luteocephalus and Ae. polynesensis* are the other species of mosquitoes incriminated as secondary vectors I Pacific Nations and Africa. Even though excellent hosts of dengue viruses, they are less efficient epidemic vectors than *Ae. aegypti*. In Australia, *Ae. aegypti, Ae.scutellaris and Ae. katherinensis* are the vectors. Species of the subgenus Finlaya (Asia) and Diceromyia (Africa) appear to be important mosquito hosts involved in dengue maintenance cycles in the forest. Two other species, *Ae. mediovittatus* shown to be excellent experimental hosts of dengue viruses.

In India, *Ae. aegypti* is the most competent primary vector in epidemic outbreaks and *Ae. albopictus, Ae. vittatus and Ae. w-albus* are the other potential vectors. *Ae.aegypti* with high anthropophillic index, is a principal vector in India and their population density fluctuate with rainfall and water storage habitats. Urbanization and migration of people have increased the habitats suitable for *Ae. aegypti* over *Ae. aegypti* over the years. This breeds in natural and artificial container such as tree holes, pots, discarded tyres, plastic containers, open tanks, air coolers etc.

Ae. albopictus, known as the 'Asian tiger' mosquito, is a species that originated from the tropical forests of Southeast Asia. Basically a sylvatic species, it creates serious public health problem because of its vectorial capacity in transmission of several arboviruses, which may be even greater than that of Ae.aegypti. Secondly, this species has the capacity to transmit the serotypes 2 and 3 of dengue virus vertically. Additionally, *Ae. albopictus* shows aggressive anthropophilic dehaviour and greater adaptability to different habitats. It breeds in tree holes, coconut shells, axils of leaves, artificial containers like plastic jars, broken pots, discarded tyres etc.

In the light of the said information and the existing endemicity of several mosquito borne disease and in particular dengue in Karnataka State, India, study of diversity of mosquitoes in forest and rural areas with respect to changing ecology was choosen. And in particular Ae.aegypti and Ae.albopictus, from forest and rural areas of Karnataka were choosen for the detailed study with respect to systematics, insecticide bioassay, isozyme studies and enzyme assay. As dengue is endemic in local situation the present investigation will add more knowledge on adaptability of mosquitoes to changing environment.

Mosquitoes go through four stages in their life-cycle: egg, larva, pupa, and adult or imago. Adult females lay their eggs in standing water, which can be a salt-marsh, a lake, a puddle, a natural reservoir on a plant, or an artificial water container such as a plastic bucket. The first three stages are aquatic and last 5-14 days, depending on the species and the ambient temperature; eggs hatch to become larvae, then pupae. The adult mosquito emerges from the pupa as it floats at the water surface. Adults live for 4-8 weeks. Mosquitoes have mouthparts that are adapted for piercing the skin of plants and animals. While males typically feed on nectar and plant juices, the female needs to obtain nutrients from a "blood meal" before she can produce eggs. There are about 3,500 species of mosquitoes found throughout the world with 41 genera. In some species of mosquito, the females feed on humans, and are therefore vectors for a number of infectious diseases affecting millions of people per year. Some scientists believe that eradicating mosquitoes would not have serious consequences for any ecosystems.

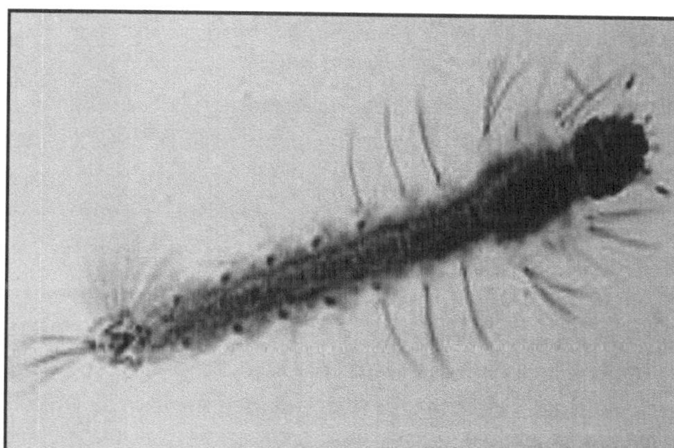

Typical *Anopheles* Larva from Mysore about 8 mm long

Mosquito larvae have a well-developed head with mouth brushes used for feeding, a large thorax with no legs and a segmented abdomen. Larvae breathe through spiracles located on the eighth abdominal segment, or through a siphon, and therefore must come to the surface frequently. The larvae spend most of their time feeding on algae, bacteria, and other micro-organisms in the surface microlayer. They dive below the surface only when disturbed. Larvae swim either through propulsion with the mouth brushes, or by jerky movements of the entire body, giving them the common name of "wigglers" or "wrigglers". Larvae develop through four stages, or instars, after which they metamorphose into pupae. At the end of each instar, the larvae molt, shedding their exoskeleton, or skin, to allow for further growth. The pupa is comma-shaped, as in *Anopheles* when viewed from the side, and is commonly called a "tumbler". The head and thorax are merged into a cephalothorax with the abdomen circling around underneath. As with the larvae, pupae must come to the surface frequently to breathe, which they do through a pair of respiratory trumpets on the cephalothorax. However, pupae do not feed during this stage. After a few days, the pupa rises to the water surface, the dorsal surface of the cephalothorax splits and the adult mosquito emerges. The pupa is less active than larva.

Adults of the yellow fever mosquitoes such as *Aedes aegypti*, a typical member of the subfamily Culicinae. The mosquitoes have black spots and the bushy antennae and longer palps in the male. The duration from egg to adult varies among species and is strongly influenced by ambient temperature. Mosquitoes can develop from egg to adult in as little as five days but usually take 10-14 days in tropical conditions. The variation of the body size in adult mosquitoes depends on the density of the larval population and food supply within the breeding water. Adult flying mosquitoes frequently rest in a tunnel that they build right below the roots of the grass. Adult mosquitoes usually mate within a few days after emerging from the pupal stage. In most species, the males form large warms, usually around dusk, and the females fly into the swarms to mate. Males live for about a week, feeding on nectar and other sources of sugar. Females will also feed on sugar sources for energy but usually require a blood meal for the development of eggs. After obtaining a full blood meal, the female will rest for a few days while the blood is digested and eggs are developed. This process depends on the temperature but usually takes 2-3 days in tropical conditions. Once the eggs are fully developed, the female lays them and resumes host seeking. The cycle repeats itself until the female dies. While females can live longer than a month in captivity, most do not live longer than 1-2 weeks in nature. Their lifespan depends on temperature, humidity, and also their ability to successfully obtain a blood meal while avoiding host defenses. Length of the adult varies but is rarely greater than 16 mm (0.6 in), and weight up to 2.5 mg (0.04 grain). All mosquitoes have slender bodies with three sections: head, thorax and abdomen.

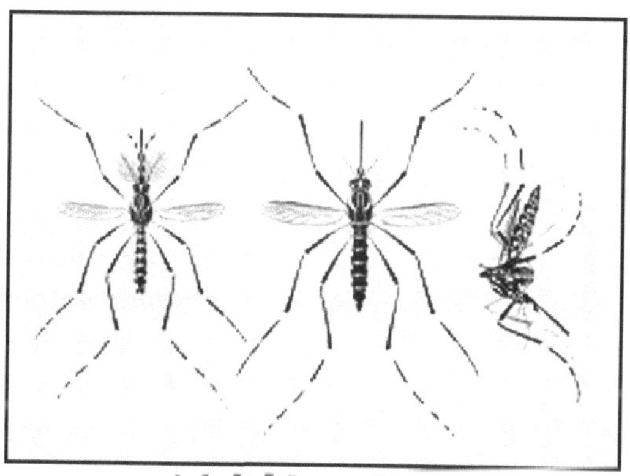

Adult Mosquitoes

The head is specialized for acquiring sensory information and for feeding. The head contains the eyes and a pair of long, many-segmented antennae. The antennae are important for detecting host odors as well as odors of breeding sites where females lay eggs. In all mosquito species, the antennae of the males in comparison to the females are noticeably bushier and contain auditory receptors to detect the characteristic whine of the female. The compound eyes are distinctly separated from one another. Their larvae only possess a pit-eye ocellus. The compound eyes of adults develop in a separate region of the head. New ommatidia are added in semicircular rows at the rear of the eye; during the first phase of growth, this leads

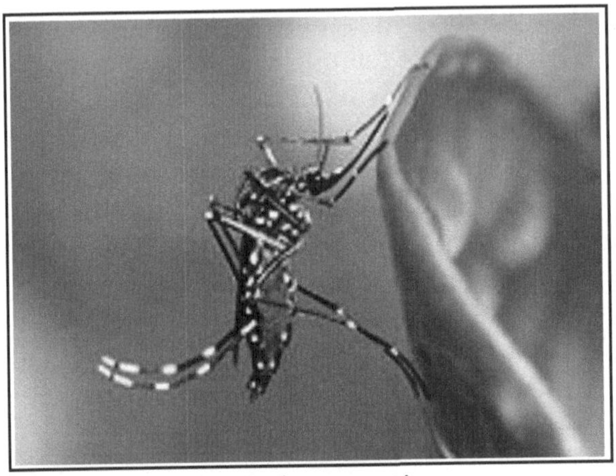

Aedes aegypti

to individual ommatidia being square, but later in development they become hexagonal. The hexagonal pattern will only become visible when the carapace of the stage with square eyes is molted. The head also has an elongated, forward-projecting "stinger-like" proboscis used for feeding, and two sensory palps. The maxillary palps of the males are longer than their proboscis whereas the females' maxillary palps are much shorter. (This is typical for representatives of subfamilies.) As with many members of the mosquito family, the female is equipped with an elongated proboscis that she uses to collect blood to feed her eggs.

The thorax is specialized for locomotion. Three pairs of legs and a pair of wings are attached to the thorax. The insect wing is an outgrowth of the exoskeleton. The *Anopheles* mosquito can fly for up to four hours continuously at 1 to 2 kilometres per hour (0.62 to 1.2 mph) travelling up to 12 km in a night. The abdomen is specialized for food digestion and egg development. This segmented body part expands considerably when a female takes a blood meal. The blood is digested over time serving as a source of protein for the production of eggs, which gradually fill the abdomen.

Feeding of mosquitoes are nectar feeders, but the females of many species are also capable of drinking blood. Females do not require blood for their own survival, but they do need supplemental substances such as protein and iron to develop eggs. With regard to host location, carbon dioxide and organic substances produced from the host, humidity, and optical recognition play important roles. In Aedes the search for a host takes place in two phases. First, the mosquito exhibits a nonspecific searching behavior until the perception of host stimulants then it follows a targeted approach. Most mosquito species are crepuscular (dawn or dusk) feeders. During the heat of the day most mosquitoes rest in a cool place and wait for the evenings, although they may still bite if disturbed. Some species, like Asian tiger mosquito, are known to fly and feed during daytime. Mosquitoes are adept at infiltration and have been known to find their way into residences via deactivated air conditioning units. Prior to and during blood feeding, they inject saliva into the bodies of their source of blood. This saliva serves as an anticoagulant: without it, the female mosquito's proboscis would quickly become clogged with blood clots. Female mosquitoes hunt their blood host by detecting carbon dioxide (CO_2) and 1-octen-3-ol from a distance. Mosquitoes of the genus *Toxorhynchites* never drink blood. This genus includes the largest extant mosquitoes, the larvae of which prey on the larvae of other mosquitoes. These mosquito eaters have been used in the past as mosquito control agents, with varying success.

Distribution of Mosquitoes

While many species are native to tropical and subtropical regions, some such as *Aedes* have successfully adapted to cooler regions. In the warm and humid tropical regions, they are active the entire year long; however, in temperate regions they hibernate over winter. Eggs from strains in the temperate zones are more tolerant to the cold than ones from warmer regions. They can even tolerate snow and sub-zero temperatures. In addition, adults can survive throughout winter in suitable microhabitats. Over large distances the worldwide distribution is carried out primarily through sea routes, in which the eggs, larvae, and pupae in combination with water-filled used tires and cut flowers are transported around. As with sea transport, the transport of mosquitoes in personal vehicles, delivery trucks, and trains plays an important role.

Anopheles albimanus mosquito feeding on a human arm. This mosquito is a vector of malaria and mosquito control is a very effective way of reducing the incidence of malaria. Mosquitoes are a vector agent that carries disease-causing viruses and parasites from person to person without catching the disease themselves. The principal mosquito borne diseases are the viral diseases yellow fever, dengue fever and Chikungunya, transmitted mostly by the *Aedes aegypti*, and malaria carried by the genus *Anopheles*. Though originally a public health concern, HIV is now thought to be almost impossible for mosquitoes to transmit. Mosquitoes are estimated to transmit disease to more than 700 million people annually in Africa, South America, Central America, Mexico and much of Asia with millions of resulting deaths. At least two million people annually die of these diseases. Methods used to prevent the spread of disease, or to protect individuals in areas where disease is endemic include Vector control aimed at mosquito eradication, disease prevention, using prophylactic drugs and developing vaccines and prevention of mosquito bites, with insecticides, nets and repellents. Since most such diseases are carried by "elderly" females, scientists have suggested focusing on these to avoid the evolution of resistance.

Development of Mosquito Egg

Two important events in the life of female mosquitoes are egg development and blood digestion. After taking a blood meal the midgut of the female synthesizes proteolytic enzymes that hydrolyze the blood proteins into free amino acids. These are used as building blocks for the synthesis of egg yolk proteins.

In the mosquito *Anopheles stephensi* Liston, trypsin activity is restricted entirely to the posterior midgut lumen. No trypsin activity occurs before the blood meal, but activity increases continuously up to 30 hours after feeding, and subsequently returns to baseline levels by 60 hours. Aminopeptidase is active in the anterior and posterior midgut regions before and after feeding. In the whole midgut, activity rises from a baseline of approximately 3 enzyme units (EU) per midgut to a maximum of 12 EU at 30 hours after the blood meal, subsequently falling to baseline levels by 60 hours. A similar cycle of activity occurs in the posterior midgut and posterior midgut lumen, whereas aminopeptidase in the posterior midgut epithelium decreases in activity during digestion. Aminopeptidase in the anterior midgut is maintained at a constant low level, showing no significant variation with time after feeding. alpha-glucosidase is active in anterior and posterior midguts before and at all times after feeding. In whole midgut homogenates, alpha-glucosidase activity increases slowly up to 18 hours after the blood meal, and then rises rapidly to a maximum at 30 hours after the blood meal, whereas the subsequent decline in activity is less predictable. All posterior midgut activity is restricted to the posterior midgut lumen. Depending upon the time after feeding, greater than 25 per cent of the total midgut activity of alpha-glucosidase is located in the anterior midgut. After blood meal ingestion, proteases are active only in the posterior midgut. Trypsin is the major primary hydrolytic protease and is secreted into the posterior midgut lumen without activation in the posterior midgut epithelium. Aminopeptidase activity is also luminal in the posterior midgut, but cellular amino-peptidases are required for peptide processing in both anterior and posterior midguts. Alpha-glucosidase activity is elevated in the posterior midgut after feeding in response to the blood meal, whereas activity in the anterior midgut is consistent with a nectar-processing role for this midgut region.

Control of Mosquito

There are many methods used for mosquito control. Depending on the situation, source reduction, biocontrol, Insecticides to kill larvae, or, to be specific, the adults may be used to manage mosquito populations. These techniques are accomplished using habitat modification, such as removing stagnant water and other breeding areas, pesticide like DDT, natural predators, (e.g. Dragonflies, larvae-eating fish), and trapping.

There are natural predators called dragonfly nymph which eats mosquitoes at all stages of development and is quite effective in controlling populations. Although bats and Purple Martins can be prodigious consumers of insects, many of which are pests, less than one per cent of their diet typically consists of mosquitoes. Neither bats nor Purple Martins are known to control or even significantly reduce mosquito populations. Some cyclopoid copepods are predators on first instar larvae, killing up to 40 Aedes larvae per day. Larval *Toxorhynchites* mosquitoes are known as natural predators of other Culicidae. Each larva can eat an average of 10 to 20 mosquito larvae per day. During its entire development, a *Toxorhynchites* larva can consume an equivalent of 5,000 larvae of the first instar (L1) or 300 fourth instar larvae (L4) (Steffan & Evenhuis, 1981; Focks, 1982). However, *Toxorhynchites* can consume all types of prey, organic debris, or even exhibit cannibalistic behavior. A number of fish are also known to consume mosquito larvae, including bass, bluegill, piranha, catfish, fathead minnows, the western mosquitofish (*Gambusia affinis*), goldfish, guppies, and killifish.

Treatment for the Mosquito Bite

Mosquito prefer some people over others. The preferential victim's sweat simply smells better than others because of the proportions of the carbon dioxide, octenol and other compounds that make up body odour. The powerful semiochemical that triggers the mosquito's keen sense of smell is nonanal. A large part of the mosquito's sense of smell, or olfactory system, is devoted to sniffing out human targets. Of 72 types of odour receptor on its antennae, at least 27 are tuned to detect chemicals found in perspiration.

Visible, irritating bites are due to an immune response from the binding of IgG and IgE antibodies to antigens in the mosquito's saliva. Some of the sensitizing antigens are common to all mosquito species, whereas others are specific to certain species. There are both immediate hypersensitivity reactions (Types I & III) and delayed hypersensitivity reactions (Type IV) to mosquito bites. There are several commercially available anti-itch medications, including those taken orally, such as Benadryl, or topically applied antihistamines and, for more severe cases, corticosteroids such as hydrocortisone and triamcinolone. Many effective home remedies exist, including calamine lotion and vinegar. A paste of meat tenderizer containing papain and water breaks down the proteins in the mosquito saliva. By using a brush to scratch the area surrounding the bite and running hot water (around 49° C) over it can alleviate itching for several hours by reducing histamine-induced skin blood flow. As a quick fix Tape or Nail polish can also be used to stabilize the bite and prevent the urge to scratch.

Index